THE USBORNE POCKET CALCULATOR BOOK

John Lewis

Edited by Helen Davies

Contents

Illustrated by Graham Round, Graham Smith, Martin Newton, Gary Rees and Martin Salisbury

Designed by Graham Round and Kim Blundell

Mathematics consultant: Nigel Langdon

Types of pocket calculators

There are lots of different types of pocket calculators ranging from simple ones that just do basic sums to scientific calculators for doing complex mathematical calculations. There are also calculators which are specially designed to do certain jobs, for instance, those used by accountants and engineers, and those which airline pilots use for navigation.

In the first part of this book you can find out how to do calculations on a simple calculator, then on pages 28-44 you can find out how to use a scientific calculator. There are lots of puzzles to solve and games to play to help improve your skill and accuracy.

Scientific calculator ▶

This kind of calculator has lots of special keys which work out complex calculations, such as sines, cosines and powers. Calculators with just a few scientific keys are sometimes called semi-scientific calculators.

On/off switch

What is the largest number you can produce using the digits 1, 2, 3, 4, 5 and the × and = keys? You can only use each digit once. (Answer on page 45.)

This is a fortune-telling calculator. It has a calendar on it and to find out your fortune on any day you enter your date of birth, then press a special key marked "Birth".

▲ Simple calculator

This is for doing everyday sums, such as adding or working out percentages. Simple calculators often have extra features, such as musical keys, or a game. Some have a built-in clock with an alarm.

Financial calculator ▲

Accountants and other business people often use a calculator like this. It has keys for working out interest on investments, depreciation, profits and losses.

▼ Programmable calculator

A programmable calculator can store the instructions for doing long, complex calculations and use them over and over again. A set of instructions is called a program. You can work out your own instructions and give them to the calculator by pressing the keys, or you can buy ready-made programs in small boxes called modules. These slot into the back of the calculator. Each module contains instructions for doing the calculations for a particular job, such as testing the strength of a bridge or navigating a boat.

These are the calculator keys.

This watch has a very small simple calculator built into it, and there is a game to play on the calculator too.

A module for a programmable calculator may contain 25 programs and up to 5000 separate instructions.

You can buy modules with games programs.

Choosing a calculator

The first thing to decide is whether you want a simple or a scientific calculator. If you are buying a simple one think about which mathematical keys you may need. If you need to work out a lot of percentages, for example, make sure the calculator has a % key. Some calculators have a memory where you can store numbers while you are doing calculations. This is very useful. You may also want a clock or a game on your calculator. If you are a student, find out which keys you will need for your work and ask in the shops about calculators specially designed for students.

A simple calculator

This picture shows a simple calculator with all the keys marked to show the jobs they do. Each job is called a function. Adding, multiplying, squaring and finding percentages are all functions.

Your calculator may not look exactly like the one shown here. It may have fewer functions and some of the symbols on the keys may be different. If so, check the instruction booklet that came with it to find out what the symbols mean.

Display panel
Most simple calculators can show eight figures in the display panel, although they may use more in their calculations.

Memory keys
These are for storing numbers in the calculator's memory. You can store the answer to one part of a sum while you work out the rest.

Percent key

Reciprocal key
You use this key to divide the number in the display into 1. This is called finding the reciprocal of the number.

Square key
Press this to square the number in the display, that is, to multiply it by itself.

Square root key
This key works out the square root of a number. The square root is the number which, when multiplied by itself would give the number you entered.

Pi key
This key puts the number 3.1415927 into the display. This number, called Pi after the Greek letter "π", is used for working out the circumference and area of circles.

Change sign key
This is for changing positive numbers into negative ones and negative numbers into positive ones. On some calculators it is labelled "CS".

Decimal point key

Equals key
Press this to finish a calculation. The answer then appears in the display.

On/off switch
Switching off the power clears all the numbers from inside the calculator.* To save batteries take care to switch off as soon as you have finished doing a sum. Some calculators switch off automatically after five minutes if no keys are pressed.

Clear key
This erases everything from inside the calculator so you can start a new calculation. It does not affect the number stored in the memory. On some calculators it is labelled "AC".

Clear entry key
This key is for correcting mistakes. It erases only the last number or instruction which you gave the calculator. On some calculators it is labelled "C".

Division key

Multiplication key

Subtraction key

Addition key

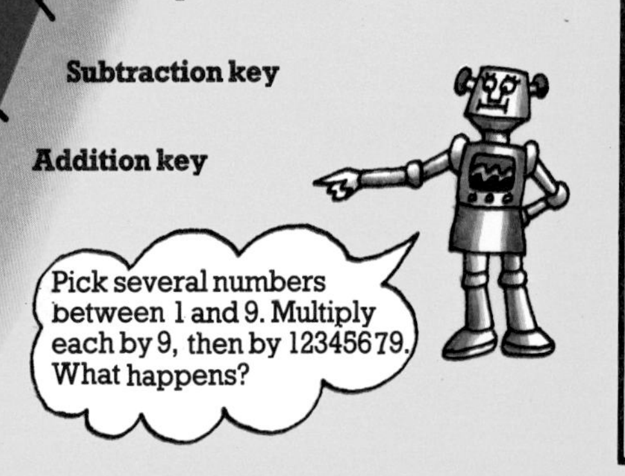

How the display works

Each digit in a calculator's display panel is made up using seven strips. The strips are arranged in a figure 8. Electrical signals from the calculator make the strips light up or change colour. By sending signals to various combinations of strips it is possible to make all the figures from 0 to 9.

In calculators with red displays the segments are made from tiny red lights called LEDs (light emitting diodes). In green displays they are made from a chemical which glows, like a fluorescent light. The black displays contain "liquid crystal" which turns black when it receives the electrical signal. Liquid crystal displays are the most common because they use least power.

Power

Most calculators use battery power. The batteries may be small torch batteries or special round ones which you can buy from calculator shops. You can also get rechargeable batteries and others which last for up to five years. Some calculators also have an adaptor and lead so they can be run from mains electricity.

This "solar-powered" calculator uses light from the sun or an ordinary room light for power. When light shines on the panel it is converted into electrical power.

*On some memory calculators the memory is not cleared when you switch off.

Doing simple sums

Here are some sums to do using the functions +, −, × and ÷, to help you get the feel of a new calculator. When you put a number into a calculator it is called entering a number. For each sum you should enter the first number, press the key for the function, enter the second number, then press the = key. In divisions make sure you enter the number you are dividing into first. Before starting each sum press the clear key to clear the previous one from the calculator.

When you are doing sums watch the calculator's display. If you enter a wrong number you can correct it by pressing the clear entry key and then entering the correct number.

1100 × 9 + 9

25 × 4

6059 × 423

The answers are on page 45.

4098 − 3097

30 ÷ 2.4 − 3

9521 − 4193

805.2 − 605.2

10.4 ÷ 2

700 × 4.3 ÷ 301

6400 ÷ 8

54 ÷ 4.5 − 6

6 × 10 × 100

9 + 17

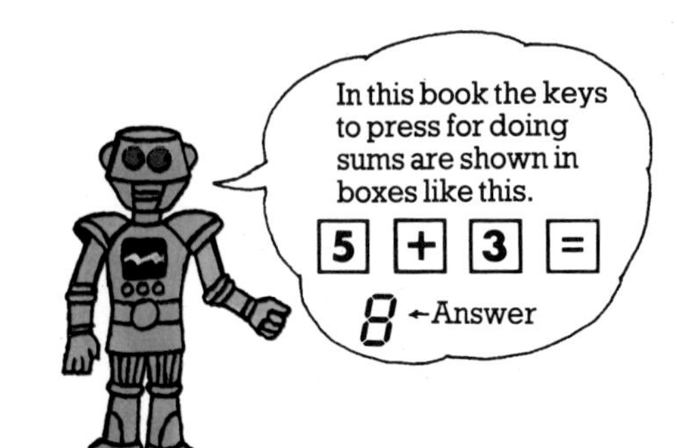

Negative numbers

Numbers such as −6 are called negative numbers because they are below zero. You can enter a negative number using the "−" key, or by pressing the change sign key (+/− or CS) after you have entered the number, as shown above.

Spotting mistakes

It is very easy to get the wrong answer on a calculator without realising it. You may enter a wrong number, or press the wrong function key. So it is a good idea to make a rough guess at the answer in your head to check the figure that the calculator gives you.

How to make a rough guess

Suppose you do the sum 1 023 × 91 and the calculator shows the answer 930 930. To make a quick check, round off the numbers to the nearest ten, hundred or thousand. In this case change 1 023 to 1 000 and 91 to 90. Then, in your head, work out 1 000 × 90. The answer is 90 000, so the calculator's figure seems too big and you should enter the sum again. In fact, the correct answer is 93 093.

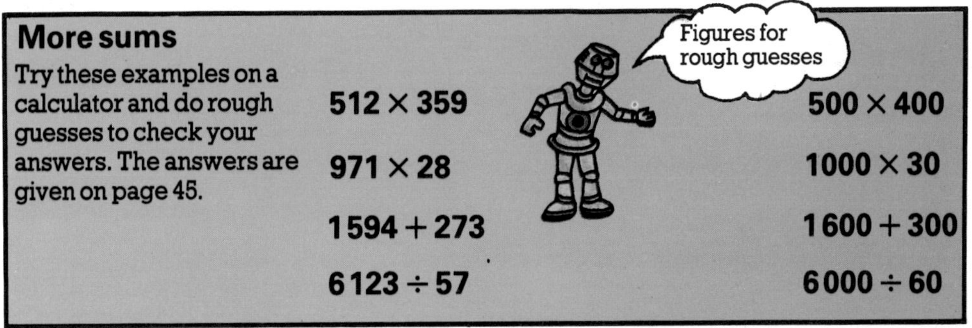

More sums

Try these examples on a calculator and do rough guesses to check your answers. The answers are given on page 45.

Sum	Figures for rough guesses
512 × 359	500 × 400
971 × 28	1000 × 30
1594 + 273	1600 + 300
6123 ÷ 57	6000 ÷ 60

Date of birth detector

Here is a trick for working out when someone was born. Ask a friend to enter into a calculator the day of the month on which they were born. Say their date of birth is 7 September 1970. They enter 7. Then you tell them to do the following:*

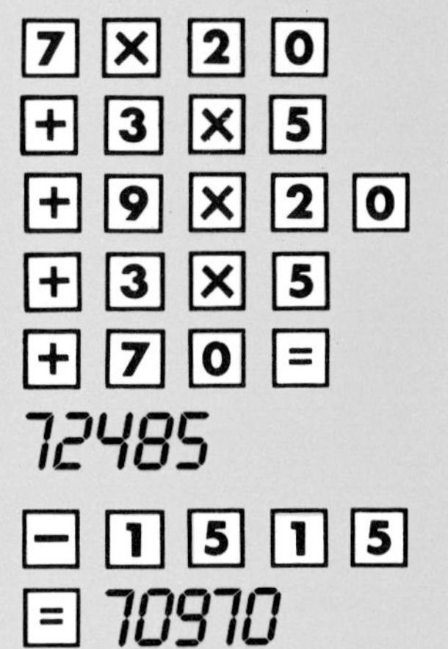

Multiply by 20, add 3 and multiply by 5.

Add on the number of the month they were born, and again multiply by 20, add 3 and multiply by 5.

Then add on the last two figures of the year in which they were born.

To work out their date of birth, take the calculator and subtract 1 515 from the number in the display. Then if you read the figures in the display from left to right, you have the day, month and year in which they were born.

*If you have a scientific calculator you may need to press = between each part of this calculation.

Car rally puzzle

Rally drivers often carry a calculator to work out how fast they should go over different sections of a race. In this puzzle you are the navigator in a rally car. The road conditions and your speed vary over the different sections of the race. Your job is to work out whether you can complete the race in the time allowed.

A

The total distance from A to the next check-point at D is 19.5km and you must be there in half an hour.

The first 9km from A to B are along a winding, hilly track and take 11.25 minutes.

B

You get stuck crossing a boggy field so your time over the next 7km from B to C is 16 minutes.

Rounding off answers

A calculator often gives a far more accurate answer than you need. For instance, if you had to divide 16 cakes amongst these 7 robots, a calculator would give the answer as 2.2857142 cakes for each robot.

It is impossible to cut cakes so accurately, so you do not need all the figures after the decimal point. Rather than just ignore them, though, you should "round off" the answer.

In most cases it is accurate enough to leave just one figure after the decimal point. To do this look at the second figure to the right of the point. If it is 5 or above, add 1 to the figure on its left. If it is 4 or below leave the figure on the left as it is.

In this example you can round the answer off to 2.3, so each robot would get about two and a third cakes.

Then at C you take a wrong turning which adds an extra 1km to your journey. In addition, the road you are on has a speed limit of 100km/h.

Can you reach the check-point on time without breaking the speed limit?

How to work it out

First you need to work out how far you still have to travel from C to D. To do this subtract the distances from A to C from the total distance; then add on the extra 1km which the wrong turning caused.

Then you need to find out how much time you have left. You know how long it took to cover the first two sections. So how many minutes do you have left? You will need to change this to hours (÷ 60) to calculate the speed in km/h.

Now, by dividing the distance left (in km) by the time left (in hours) you can work out what speed you must do to reach the check-point in time. Will you break the speed limit? The answer is on page 45.

Remember the speed you work out is your average speed. You are unlikely to be able to travel at exactly this all the way. You will go below and above it.

Another car which set out from A at the same time as you reached the check-point 5 minutes before you. What was its average speed? (Answer on page 45.)

Doing sums with fractions

1 ÷ 2 =

Keys to press to convert ½.

0.5

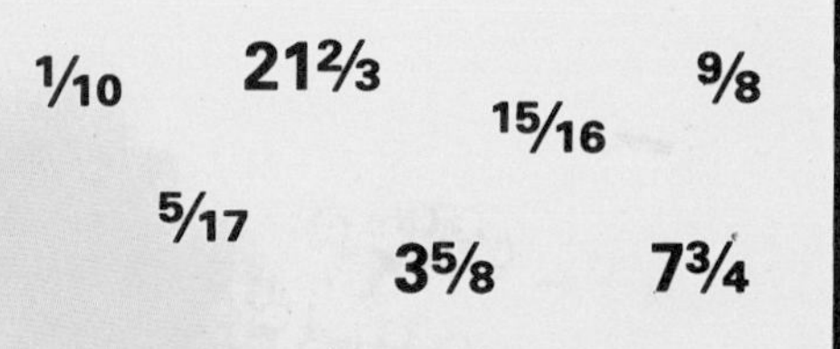

Most calculators cannot work in fractions so you have to convert them to decimals. To do this you divide the top part of the fraction by the bottom part.

To convert mixed numbers which have fractions and whole numbers (for example, $3\frac{11}{16}$), you only need to work out the fraction part because the whole number does not change. ($11 \div 16 = 0.6875$ so $3\frac{11}{16} = 3.6875$).

Can you convert these fractions to decimals? The answers are on page 45.

When you are doing sums you should not round off the numbers until the very end. You should always use all the figures after the decimal point for the calculations.

Inside a calculator

This picture shows the parts inside a calculator where the calculations are done. When you press the keys to enter the numbers and functions for a sum, electrical signals are sent inside the calculator and the numbers and functions are converted into a special code which the calculator uses for doing calculations. Below you can find out how the calculator does a simple sum.

① Scanners
When the calculator is on, these constantly search the keyboard, waiting to pick up the electrical signal made when a key is pressed.

② Encoder unit
This is where the numbers and functions are converted into the code which the calculator uses for doing sums.

④ Flag register
The function for the calculation is stored here until the calculator needs it.

⑥ Permanent memory
The instructions telling the calculator how to add, subtract, do percentages, square roots and all the other functions it can carry out are stored here. The instructions are called programs and they are put in the permanent memory when the calculator is made.

A simple sum

Imagine you are doing the sum 23 + 7. When you enter 23 it is picked up by scanners ①, coded ② and sent to the X register ③.

Next you press the + and this is also picked up by the scanners and coded. Then it is sent to the flag register ④.

The second number, 7, is coded and sent to the X register. This pushes the first number out into the Y register ⑤.

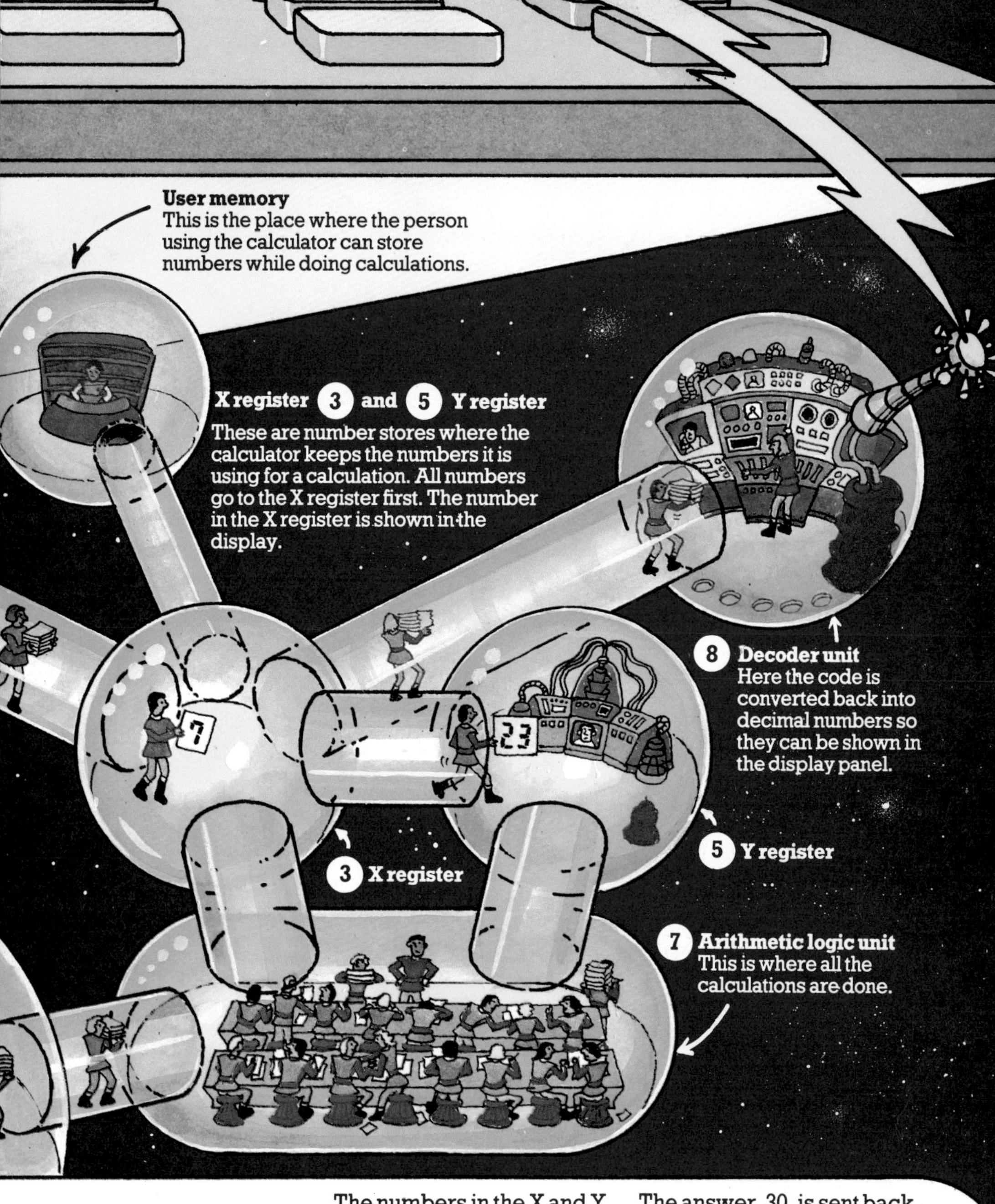

When you press = a message from the flag register tells the permanent memory ⑥ that the sum is an addition.

The numbers in the X and Y registers are then loaded into the arithmetic logic unit ⑦ and the calculation is carried out following instructions from the permanent memory.

The answer, 30, is sent back to the X register. From there it goes to the decoder unit ⑧. It is converted into a decimal number and then shown in the display.

Calculator code

The code which the calculator uses for doing sums is made up of pulses of electricity. There are two signals in the code: pulse and no-pulse. It is called a binary code and can be expressed in numbers with a "0" for no-pulse and a "1" for pulse. Different arrangements of the signals are used to represent the numbers, the functions and all the other information in a calculator.

No-pulse

Pulse

The patterns of signals are controlled by tiny electronic components called transistors. These act like gates, opening to let electric pulses through and shutting to stop them.

Number codes

The numbers we use (0-9) are in decimal code. Below you can see the difference between decimal and binary number codes.

Decimal code

In decimal code there are ten digits: 0123456789. When you write a number, each digit represents a set of units. The right-hand digit represents 1s. Each time you move to the left the size of the units increases ten times. So, in the number 3 507 there are seven 1s, no 10s, five 100s and three 1 000s.

1000s	100s	10s	1s
3	5	0	7

3000 + 500 + 0 + 7 = 3507

Added together this makes three thousand, five hundred and seven.

More about transistors

Inside a calculator there are hundreds of thousands of transistors. The transistors are linked together in pathways, called circuits, along which the electric pulses travel. The circuits containing transistors are engraved by a special chemical process onto a tiny chip of a substance called silicon. The chip of silicon is called an integrated circuit, or just a "chip".

The chips of silicon are enclosed in plastic cases like the ones shown here. The metal legs carry the electric current from the battery into and out of the chip.

Binary code

In binary code there are only two digits. When you write a number the right-hand digit represents 1s and each time you move to the left the size of the units doubles. So in the binary number 1011 there is one 1, one 2, no 4s and one 8.

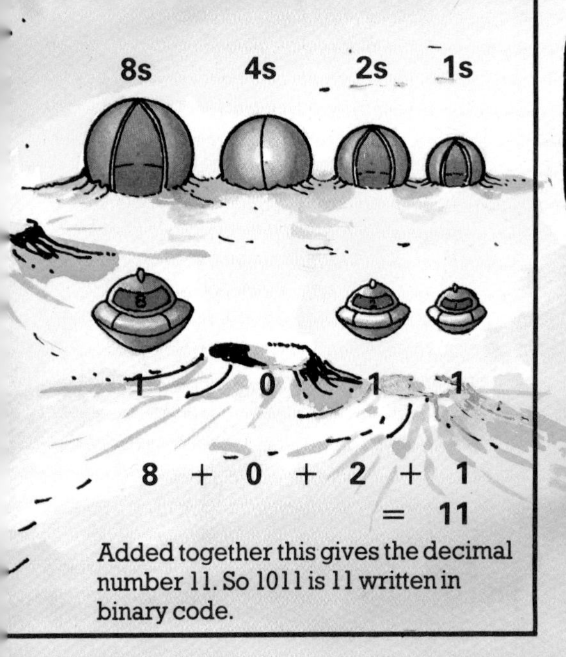

Added together this gives the decimal number 11. So 1011 is 11 written in binary code.

Binary decoder

Here is an easy way to decode binary numbers into decimal ones.

Imagine you have a row of lightbulbs numbered 8, 4, 2, 1. If the switch below a bulb is down, the light is on and it represents a binary 1.

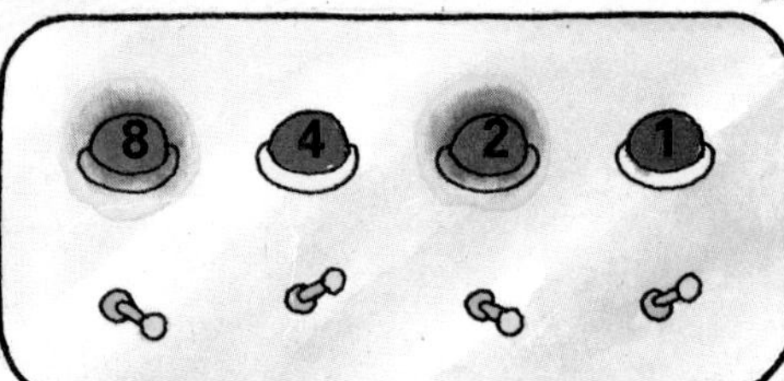

To decode a binary number, say 1010, start from the right of the binary number and for each binary 1 switch on the corresponding light on the decoder. Then add up the numbers on the bulbs that are lit to get the answer in decimal numbers. Can you decode the binary numbers shown below?

0011 **1111** **0101**

0111 **1100** **1001**

The answers are on page 45.

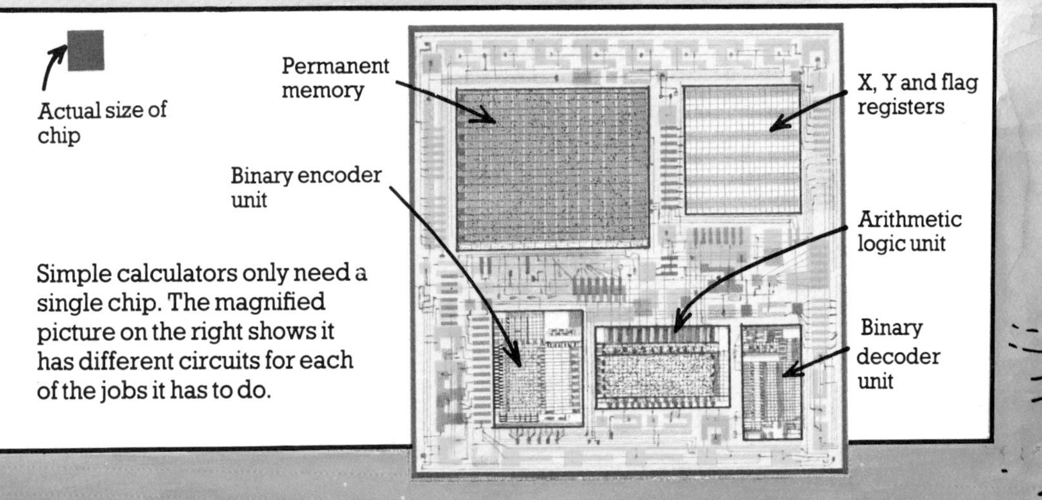

Simple calculators only need a single chip. The magnified picture on the right shows it has different circuits for each of the jobs it has to do.

How a calculator works out sums

Did you know that a calculator does all its calculations just by adding? This is the only mathematical process it can carry out in binary. It does multiplications, square roots and every other calculation by adding the numbers according to sets of rules stored in its permanent memory. Below you can see how a calculator works out 6 × 5.

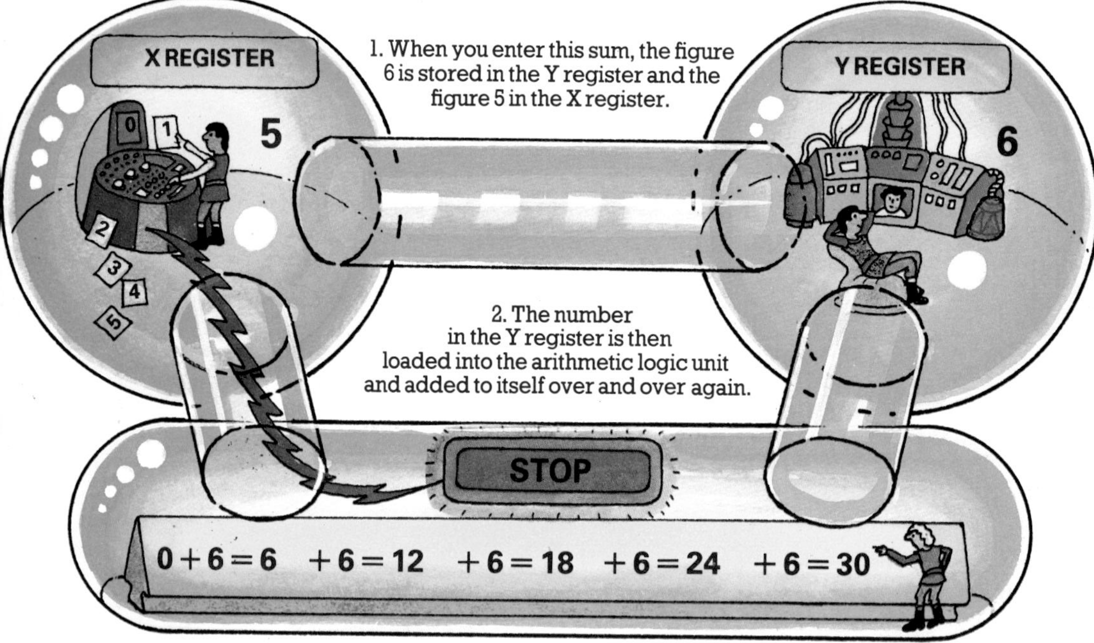

1. When you enter this sum, the figure 6 is stored in the Y register and the figure 5 in the X register.

2. The number in the Y register is then loaded into the arithmetic logic unit and added to itself over and over again.

3. The number in the X register shows how many times the addition should be done. Each time 6 is added to itself the X register number is reduced by 1.

4. When the number in the X register reaches zero a message tells the arithmetic logic unit to stop adding and the calculation is complete.

Every calculation the calculator does has to be reduced to simple steps which involve only adding. The rules for each calculation are called algorithms and they are worked out by the engineers and mathematicians who design calculators. The rules for multiplication are simple compared with those for square roots and other scientific functions, which may have hundreds of steps.

Calculator versus brain race

A calculator works so quickly that you do not notice how many steps it has to perform to do a sum. However, if you are good at mental arithmetic you may be able to beat the calculator. Ask someone to work out the sums on the right on a calculator while you do them in your head. Both start at the same moment. Can you do them faster than the calculator?

4 × 12	4 × 7 + 5
9 + 46	9 + 8 − 3
175 − 50	73 − 17 + 16
70 × 5	244 ÷ 2 + 15
108 ÷ 12	2 × 2 + 46

You can check your answers on page 45.

Number tricks

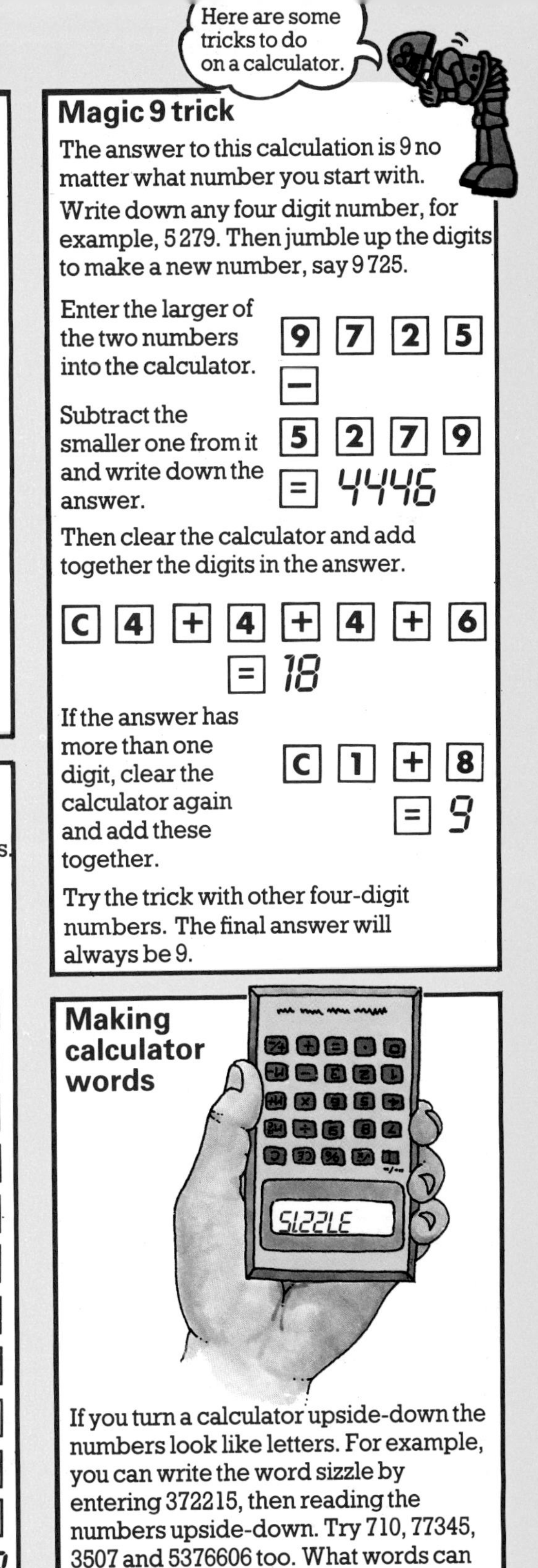

13 trick

This calculation gives the answer 13 whatever number you start with.

Think of any three-digit number, for example, 853

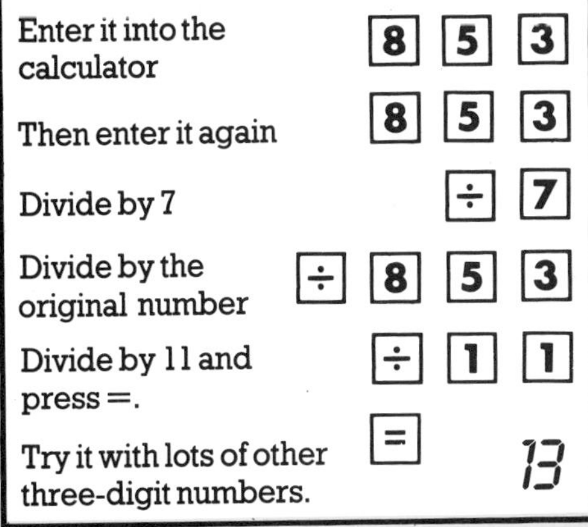

Enter it into the calculator	8 5 3
Then enter it again	8 5 3
Divide by 7	÷ 7
Divide by the original number	÷ 8 5 3
Divide by 11 and press =.	÷ 1 1
Try it with lots of other three-digit numbers.	= 13

Guess the number

Ask a friend to think of any number and write it down, without telling you what it is. Then give them the calculator and tell them to do the following:*

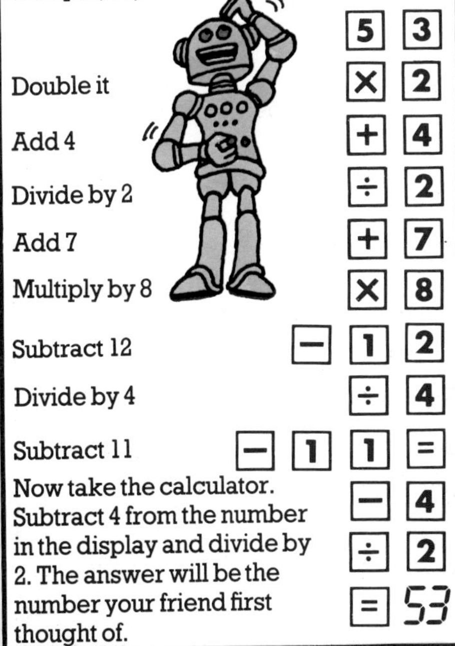

Enter the number (for example, 53)	5 3
Double it	× 2
Add 4	+ 4
Divide by 2	÷ 2
Add 7	+ 7
Multiply by 8	× 8
Subtract 12	− 1 2
Divide by 4	÷ 4
Subtract 11	− 1 1 =
Now take the calculator. Subtract 4 from the number in the display and divide by 2. The answer will be the number your friend first thought of.	− 4 ÷ 2 = 53

Magic 9 trick

The answer to this calculation is 9 no matter what number you start with.

Write down any four digit number, for example, 5 279. Then jumble up the digits to make a new number, say 9 725.

Enter the larger of the two numbers into the calculator.	9 7 2 5
Subtract the smaller one from it and write down the answer.	− 5 2 7 9 = 4446

Then clear the calculator and add together the digits in the answer.

C 4 + 4 + 4 + 6 = 18

If the answer has more than one digit, clear the calculator again and add these together.	C 1 + 8 = 9

Try the trick with other four-digit numbers. The final answer will always be 9.

Making calculator words

SIZZLE

If you turn a calculator upside-down the numbers look like letters. For example, you can write the word sizzle by entering 372215, then reading the numbers upside-down. Try 710, 77345, 3507 and 5376606 too. What words can you make?

*If you have a scientific calculator you may have to press = after each part of this calculation.

Using the memory

When you are doing calculations you often need to remember the answer to part of a calculation so you can use it again later on. Most calculators have a memory where you can store a number during a calculation. It is usually operated by three keys, labelled M+, M−, MR. Two other keys are described below. If the memory keys on your calculator are labelled differently check the instruction booklet to see what each one does.

The memory is an extra number store attached to the X register (see the picture on pages 10-11). It contains only zeros until you store a number in it. On most simple calculators the memory is erased when you switch off the calculator.

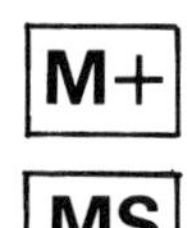

This key puts the number in the display into the memory. If there is a number already in the memory, the new number is added to it. Some calculators have an MS or "memory store" key. This puts the number in the display into the memory and erases any number already there.

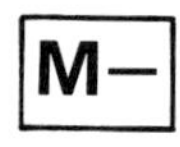

This subtracts the number in the display from the number in the memory.

This is the memory recall key. It puts the number in the memory into the display so you can use it in the sum you are doing. The number is still stored in the memory though, so you can use it again if necessary.

The memory clear key erases a number from the memory. Some calculators have no memory clear key and to clear the memory you press MR followed by M−, or on some calculators, the ordinary clear key, followed by MS.

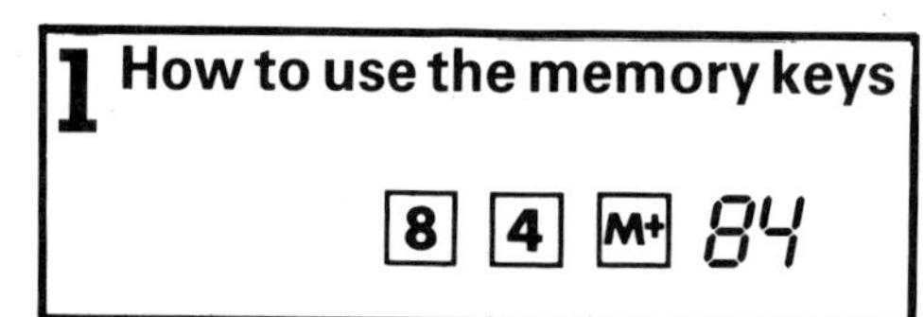

To store a number, for instance, 84, in the memory first enter it into the calculator, then press M+ or MS. If you use the M+ key to store a number make sure the memory is clear before you start.

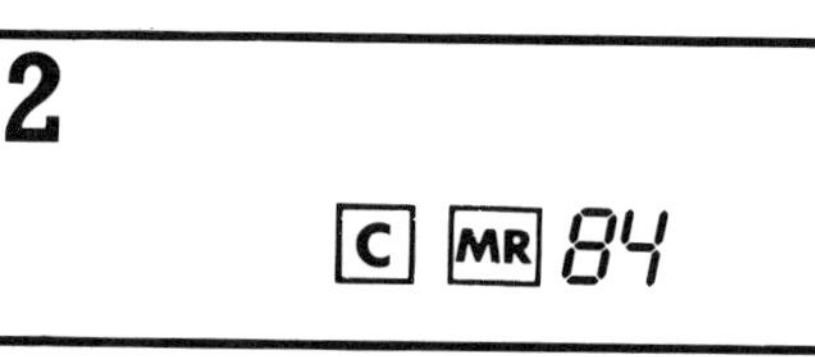

Press C to clear the display. Then check the number is still in the memory by pressing MR. The number appears in the display and it is also retained in the memory.

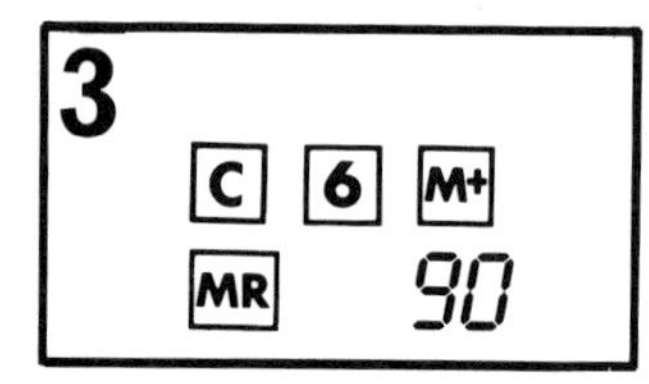

To add a number to the one in the memory enter it and then press M+. Press MR to see the new total.

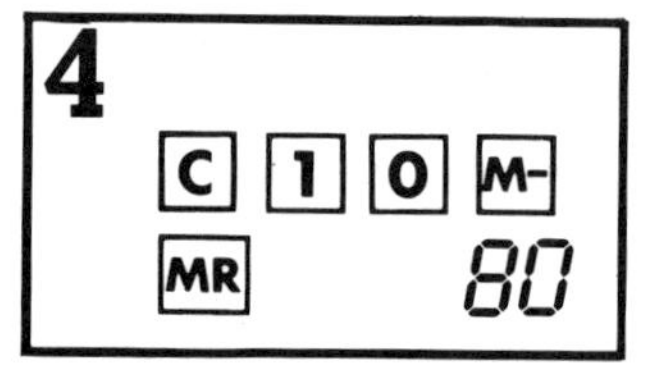

To subtract a number from the one in the memory enter it and then press M−. To check the new total in the memory press MR.

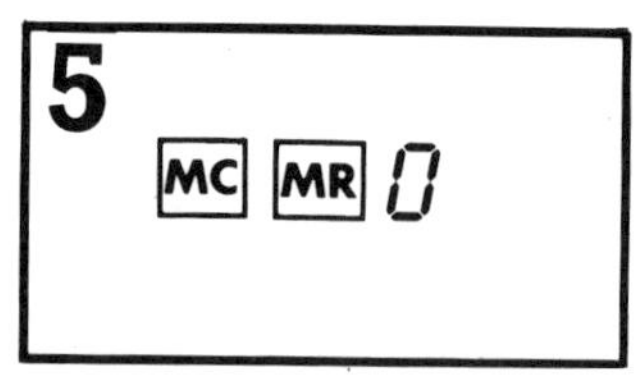

Clear the memory. Now if you press the MR key, a zero will appear in the display.

Memory sums

These examples show how you can use the memory to make calculations with several parts easier to solve. You can only store one number at a time in the memory so plan your calculations carefully. In divisions or subtractions you need to work out the second part of the sum first and store the answer in the memory so that you are dividing into or subtracting from the right part of the sum. There is an example like this in box 1. Before you start check that the calculator and the memory are clear.

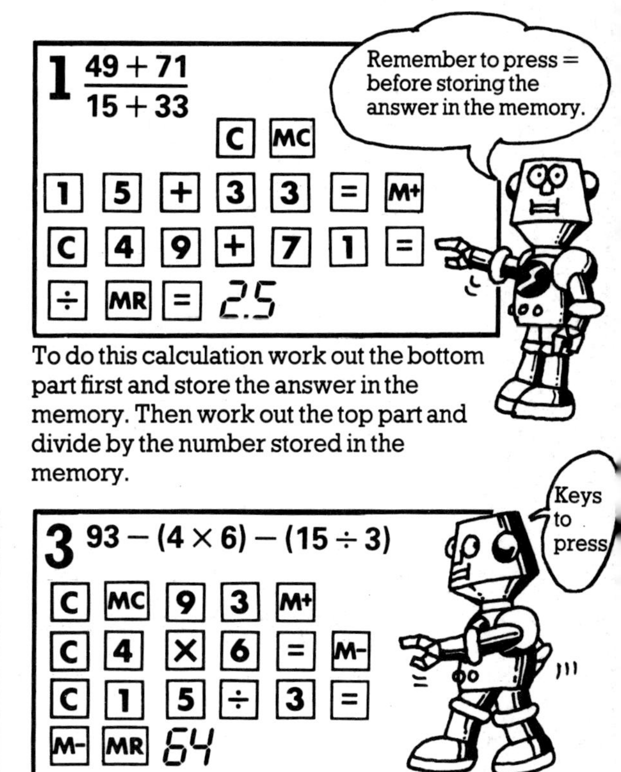

To do this calculation work out the bottom part first and store the answer in the memory. Then work out the top part and divide by the number stored in the memory.

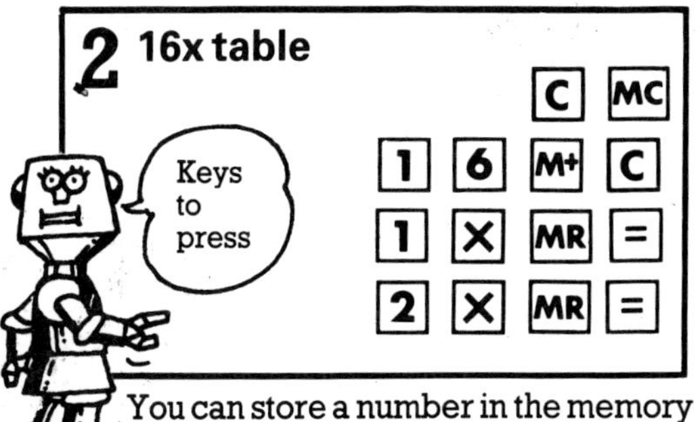

You can store a number in the memory to save entering it over and over again. For instance, to work out the 16× table store 16 in the memory, then press MR each time you multiply.

One way to do this calculation is to put 93 in the memory, then work out each of the sums in brackets and subtract the answers from 93 using the M− key. To get the final answer press MR.

Mountaineer puzzle

This mountaineer must not carry more than 17kg on his back. His rucksack with a tent, sleeping bag and climbing equipment weighs 11.75kg. To this he adds: cooking equipment weighing 2kg, two packets of rice weighing 430g each, seven packets of dried soup weighing 85g each, three packets of tea weighing 113g each, five sachets of milk powder weighing 21g each.

Then he remembers he should take some chocolate. Each bar weighs 103g. How many can he carry without exceeding his weight limit? Remember 1kg = 1 000g. The answer is on page 45.

Another kind of memory

Many simple calculators have another kind of memory called the constant function. This memory is automatic and there is no key to operate it. To check whether your calculator has a constant enter 5 + 2, then press =. The answer, 7, appears. Now press the = key again. If the answer changes to 9, the +2 part of the sum has been stored in the constant. It will be added to the figure in the display each time you press =. The constant is useful in sums where you need to perform the same function over and over again.

Below you can find out how to use the constant in calculations. Then you can see how to use it for doing conversions and for count-downs and keeping a tally.

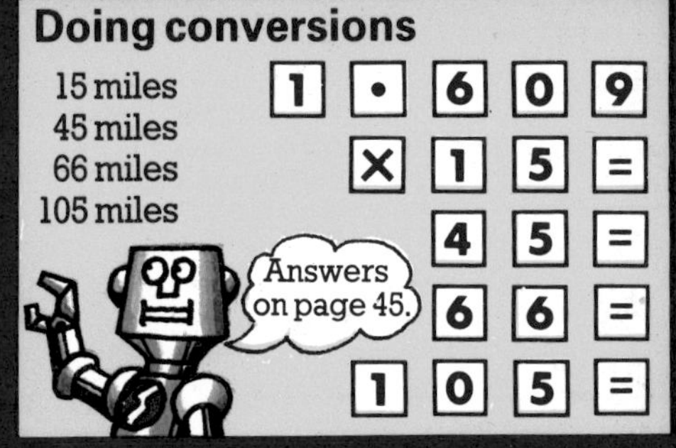

One mile is 1.609km, so to convert these distances to kilometres you multiply them by 1.609. When you do the first sum 1.609 is stored as a constant and to multiply the other numbers you enter them, then press =.*

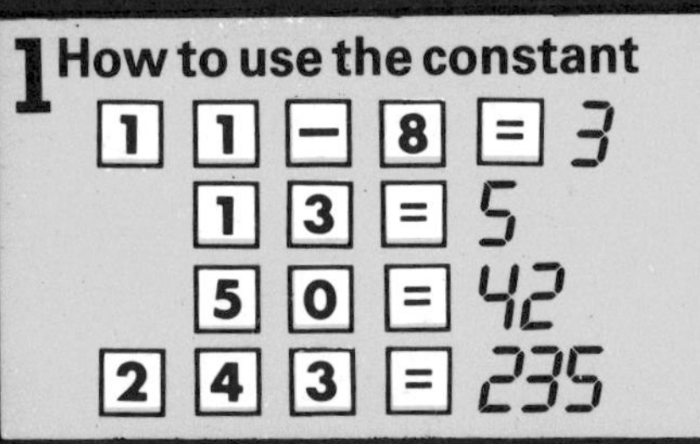

Suppose you want to subtract 8 from 11, 13, 50 and 243. When you enter the first numbers, the −8 is stored in the constant. To subtract 8 from the other numbers, enter each number, then press =.

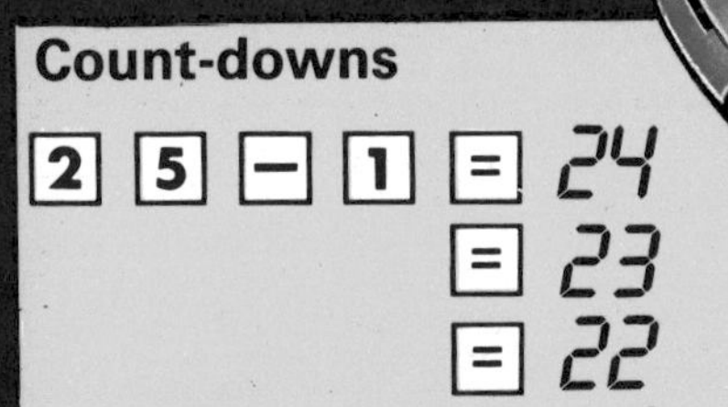

You can make a count-down by storing −1 in the constant. For example to count down 25 seconds to the start of a race enter 25 − 1, then press = each time a second passes.

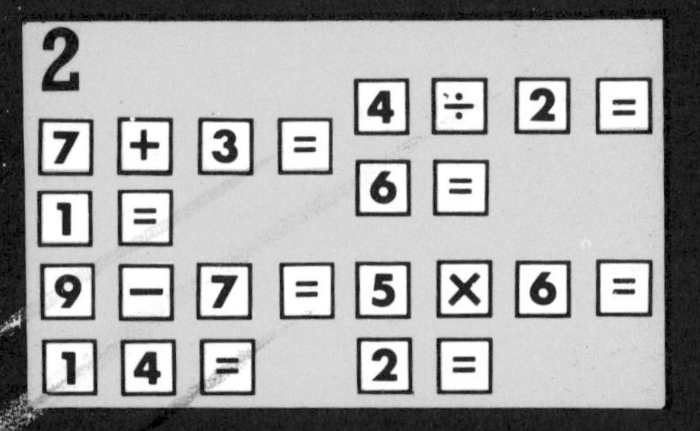

Most calculators store the second part of an addition, subtraction or division in the constant, but the first part of a multiplication. Try the above examples to see how your calculator works.

Making a tally

+ 1 =

=

=

=

A tally is the opposite of a count-down. You could make a tally of the number of cars passing your house by entering +1, then pressing = each time a car passes.

*If your calculator stores the second part of a multiplication in the constant, you need to enter the first sum the other way round.

Space invader puzzle

Can you solve this puzzle? If your calculator has memory keys, try to do it without writing down any part of the calculations.

You are trying to beat a friend at space invaders. Their score is 18 950. You manage to knock out 151 invaders, 19 rockets, 5 flying saucers and the command ship. The scoring system is: 20 points for an invader, 330 points for a rocket, 550 points for a flying saucer and 5 000 points for the command ship.

Have you beaten your friend? What is the difference between your scores? (Answers on page 45.)

Change sign key

If your calculator does not have memory keys you can use the change sign key (the key which changes positive numbers to negative ones and vice versa) to do sums such as the one shown here.

Work out the second part of the sum first. Then you have to subtract the answer from 50. To do this press the change sign key to make the number in the display negative. Now add 50. The calculation $-12 + 50$ gives the same answer as $50 - 12$.

Error alert

Most calculators have a warning device to tell you if something is wrong. For instance, it is impossible to divide a number by 0. If you try to do so on a calculator an E standing for error, or a zero (sometimes flashing) appears in the display.

On most calculators the warning also appears if the answer to a calculation is too big or too small to be shown in the display. For example, if you try to divide 0.000 006 by 1 000 or multiply 5 000 000 by 20 000.

Working out percentages

If your calculator has a percent key (marked %) you can do percentages very easily and also work out percentage increases and reductions.

A percentage is a special kind of fraction. For example, 3% of 40 is the same as $\frac{3}{100}$ of 40 and 25% of 70 is $\frac{25}{100}$ (= $\frac{1}{4}$) of 70. The keys to press to work these out on a calculator are shown on the right.

How to use the % key

To work out a percentage of a number, you enter the number, then multiply by the percentage you want and press the percent key.

% increases and % reductions

Below you can find out how to work out percentage increases and reductions on a calculator. These calculations are useful for working out, say, the price of an item that has been reduced by 20% or how to add 10% service charge to a bill. You do these sums in different ways on different calculators. To find out which way you should use try these examples and check your answers with those given here.

1

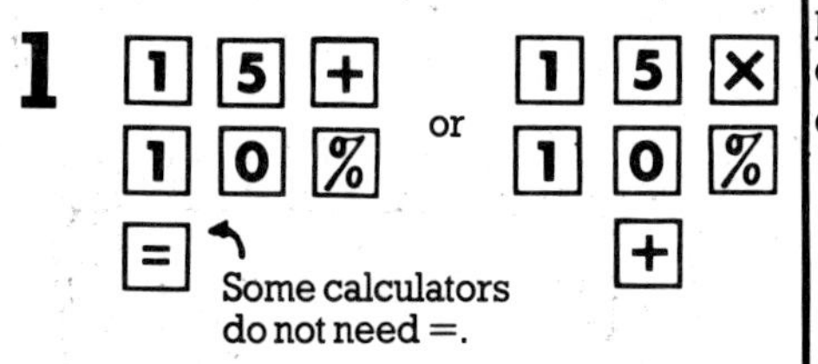

Here are the two ways to work out a 10% increase on 15. The answer should be 16.5.

2

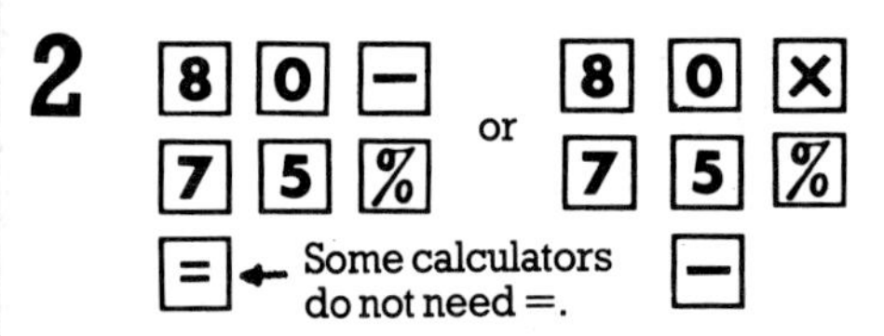

These are the two different sets of keys to press to reduce 80 by 75%. The answer should be 20.

Converting fractions to percentages

Keys to press	Answers
3 ÷ 4 %	75 %
2 ÷ 3 %	66.7 %
5 ÷ 8 %	62.5 %

On some calculators you can use the % key to change fractions to percentages. The keys to press to change $\frac{3}{4}$ to a percentage are shown above. Try working out $\frac{2}{3}$ and $\frac{5}{8}$ too to see how it works on your calculator.

Hats puzzle

In the picture below can you work out what percentage of the robots have blue hats, what percentage have red hats and what percentage have yellow hats? Round off the percentages to whole numbers. (Answers on page 46.)

If you add up the three percentages the answer should be 100%. In fact it is only 99% because rounding off makes the percentages slightly inaccurate.

Galactic spore puzzle

Planet Zanof has been invaded by a deadly weed – a spore from galactic space. The Zanof scientists are desperately trying to find a herbicide to destroy it, but the weed has already covered ⅕ of the planet, and every day the area it covers increases by 33%. How many days do the scientists have left, before it overruns the whole planet?

Hints for working it out

The planet will be completely overrun when the weed covers 100% of it. At present the weed covers 20% (= ⅕), so enter 20 into the calculator and add 33% to it. Keep increasing the number in the display by 33% until it reaches just less than 100. The number of times you add 33% is the number of days they have left. You can check your answer on page 46.

Percentages without a % key

Here is an easy way to work out percentages if your calculator does not have a % key. Below you can find out how to work out 20% of 16.

$$20\% = \frac{20}{100} = 0.2$$

To work out this sum first you have to convert the percentage to a decimal figure by dividing it by 100. An easy way to do this is to move the decimal point two places to the left, i.e. 20% is 0.2.

= 3.2

Then to work out 20% of 16 multiply 16 by the decimal number as shown above. See if you can work out the following percentages without using the % key: 25% of 5 800, 35% of 675, 115% of 50, 46% of 900. (Answers on page 46.)

Squares and square roots

On these two pages you can find out how to use the square and square root keys on a calculator. Squaring a number means multiplying it by itself, and the symbol for squaring is a small 2 beside the number (for example, 4^2). On a calculator the square key is labelled x^2.

A square root is the opposite of a square. The label on the square root key is $\sqrt{\ }$ or $\sqrt{x}$.

1 Doing squares

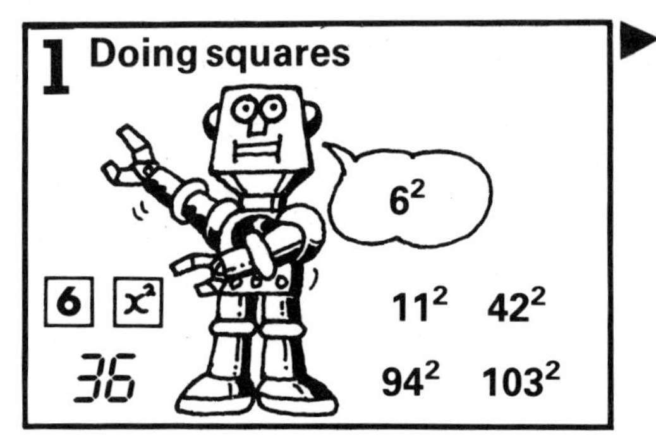

To square a number, for instance 6, enter it, then press the x^2 key. You should not press =. Can you work out the squares of the other numbers shown above? The answers are on page 46.

Doing square roots

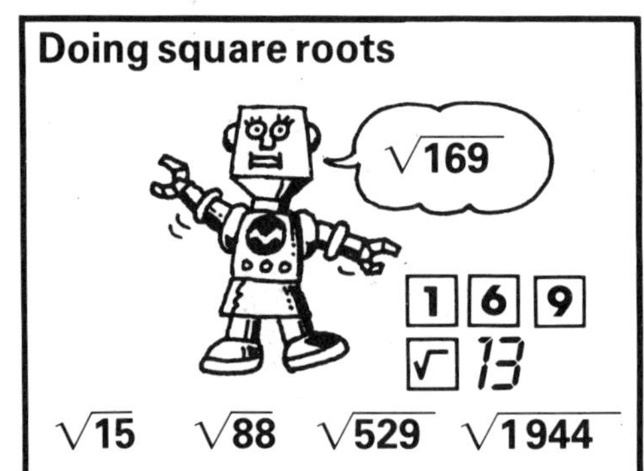

$\sqrt{15}$ $\sqrt{88}$ $\sqrt{529}$ $\sqrt{1944}$

To find the square root of a number you enter it, then press the $\sqrt{\ }$ key. Try the examples above. The answers are on page 46.

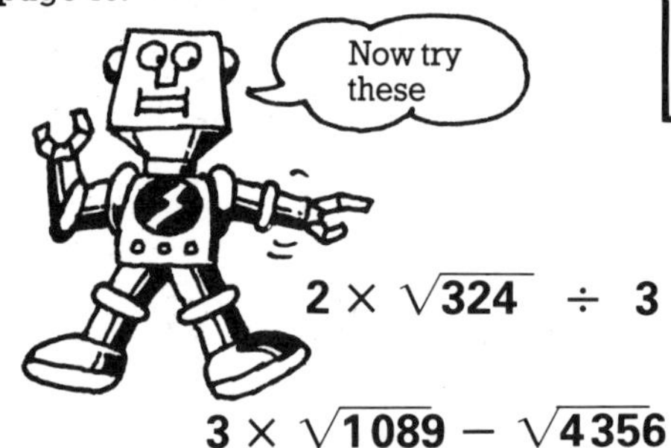

$2 \times \sqrt{324} \div 3$

$3 \times \sqrt{1089} - \sqrt{4356}$

$9555 \div \sqrt{5402.25}$

In these calculations you can work out each square root as you come to it, but remember, always enter the number first, then press the $\sqrt{\ }$ key.

Square number tricks

Here are some tricks and puzzles to try. They all involve squaring numbers.

Reappearing squares puzzle

$5^2 = 25 \quad 6^2 = 36 \quad 25^2 = 625$

Above there are three numbers which when squared reappear as the last figure or figures in the answer.

There are only three other numbers between 25 and 1 000 which do this. Can you work out which they are? The answers are on page 46.

Hint: note that the numbers already given all end with a figure 5 or 6.

Time your reactions

How quickly can you catch a falling object? Here is a test to find out. You need a ruler, a calculator and a friend to help you.

1

Ask your friend to hold the ruler with the 0cm mark pointing down. Hold your thumb and finger round the ruler at the 0cm mark without actually touching the ruler. Then tell your friend to drop the ruler without warning you.

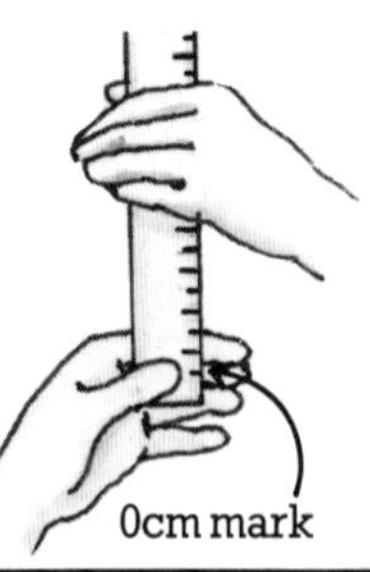

2

0.2^2
0.65^2
0.83^2
0.9^2

If a number is less than 1, squaring it makes it smaller. Try the examples above. The answers are on page 46.

3 $1734 \div 17^2 - 5$

[1] [7] [3] [4]
[÷] [1] [7] [x^2]
[−] [5] [=] 1

This example shows how to work out squares in the middle of a calculation.

4

7^2
[7] [×] [=] 49
18^2
[1] [8] [×] [=] 324

If you do not have an x^2 key you can work out squares by doing a normal multiplication, or you can use the constant* as shown here.

Back to square one

Here is a squaring sum to which the answer is always the number you started with.

Enter any number into the calculator, square it and store the result in the memory (or write it down).

[4] [1] [x^2] [M+]

Then enter the original number plus 1, and square that.

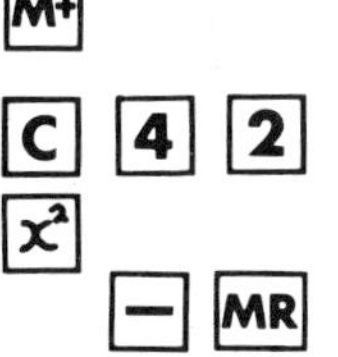

[C] [4] [2] [x^2]

Subtract the square of the first number (which is in the memory).

[−] [MR]

Then subtract 1, and divide by 2.

[−] [1] [÷] [2] [=] 41

Now try other numbers.

5^2 trick

Enter any number ending in 5. Square it, then store the result in the memory.

[6] [5] [x^2] [M+]

Now enter the number again without the figure 5 and multiply it by the next biggest number. Write down the answer.

[C] [6] [×] [7] [=] 42

Then tack on 25 (which is 5^2). This number is the square of the number you first entered. Press MR to check it.

4225

[MR] 4225

2

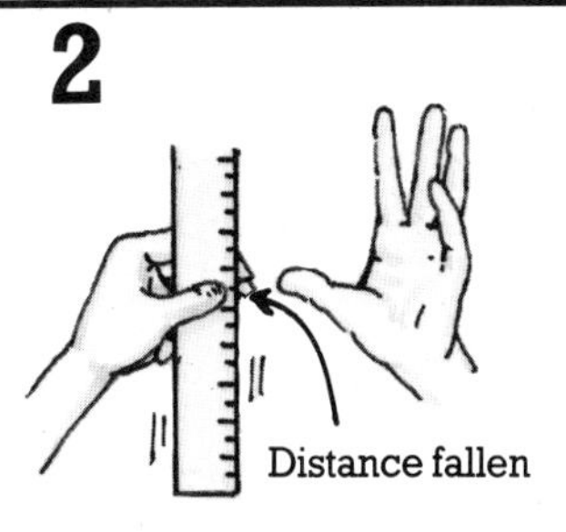

As soon as the ruler falls, catch it and note where your thumb and finger are gripping it. This shows the distance it has fallen.

Calculating your reaction time

Suppose the distance is 19.5cm. Your reaction time is the time it took the ruler to fall this distance. Since the ruler is falling under the pull of gravity its acceleration is 980cm/sec^2. So you can work out the time using the following mathematical formula:

$$\text{Time}^2 = 2\left(\frac{\text{distance}}{\text{acceleration}}\right)$$

Keys to press

[1] [9] [•] [5] [÷] [9] [8] [0] [×] [2]
[=] 0.0397959

The answer is the time^2, so the time is $\sqrt{0.0397959}$, which is 0.2 seconds. This is quite a slow reaction time. Is yours better?

*See page 18.

More square puzzles over the page. ▶

Square puzzles

The square and square root keys are useful for working out measurements of triangles using Pythagoras' theorem. Pythagoras' theorem states that on a right-angled triangle the square of the long side (called the hypotenuse) is equal to the sum of the squares of the other two sides. You can check this on the triangle below.

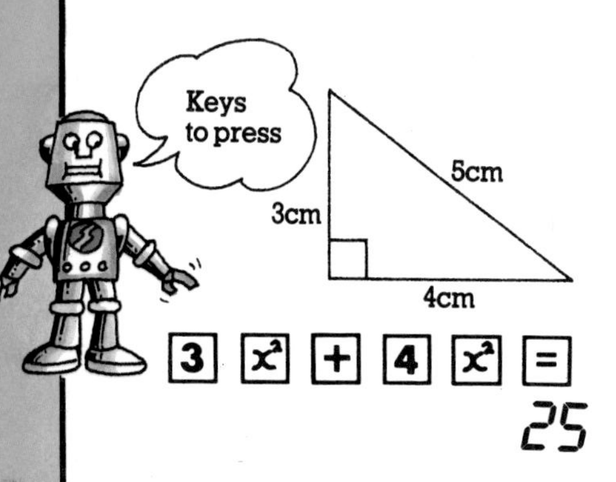

Now see if you can solve these puzzles. The answers are on page 46.

Slim Sally's CB aerial

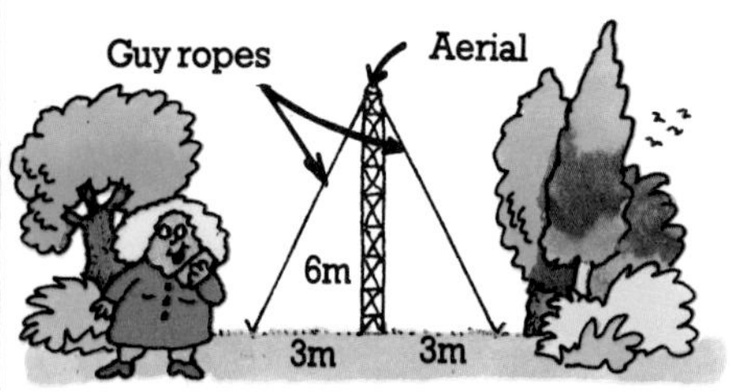

Sally has a CB aerial in her garden. The aerial is 6m high and her garden is 6m wide. How long are the guy ropes?

Walking puzzle

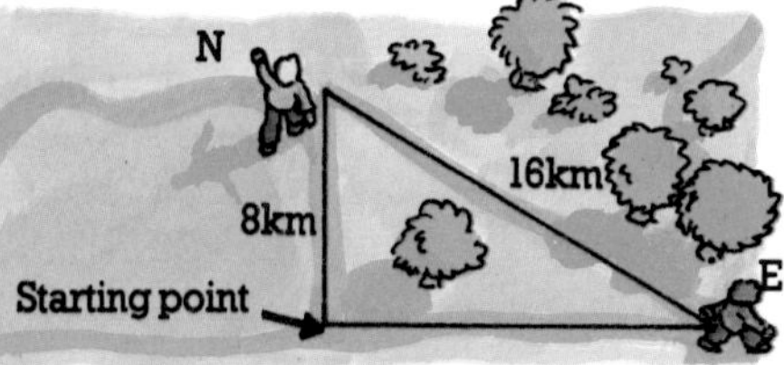

Jim and Lee set off walking from the same point. Jim walks due North and Lee due East. When Jim has walked 8km he is 16km from Lee. How far has Lee walked?

Star warrior puzzle

The evil Toron has captured an electric star warrior and imprisoned him in a water chamber. When the chamber is full the water will touch the warrior and electrocute him. The main pipe takes 9 minutes to fill the chamber, but the Toron sees a rescue ship coming so he turns on a second pipe as well. This takes 24 minutes to fill the chamber. The rescuers arrive after 6 minutes – are they in time?

Hints for working it out

One way to solve the puzzle is to work out how long it takes to fill the chamber using both pipes. Say it takes n minutes, then in one minute $1/n$ of the chamber is filled. You know that one pipe fills the chamber in 9 minutes, so in one minute it fills $1/9$ of the chamber. The other pipe fills $1/24$ of the chamber in one minute. So $1/n = 1/9 + 1/24$. To work out sums like this some calculators have a key which automatically divides numbers into 1. It is called the reciprocal key and labelled "$1/x$". You can use it to work out

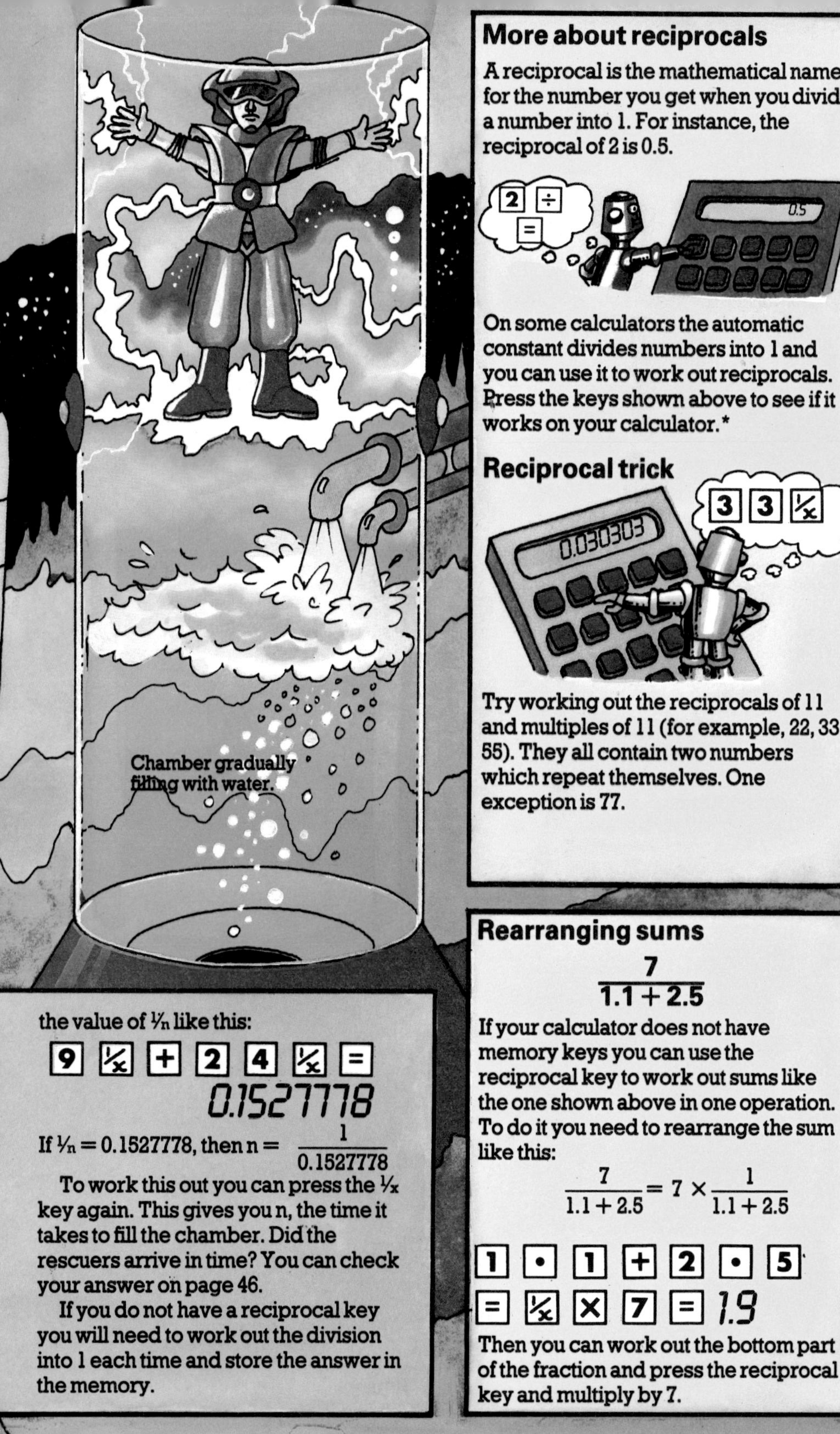

the value of $1/n$ like this:

[9] [1/x] [+] [2] [4] [1/x] [=]

0.1527778

If $1/n = 0.1527778$, then $n = \frac{1}{0.1527778}$

To work this out you can press the $1/x$ key again. This gives you n, the time it takes to fill the chamber. Did the rescuers arrive in time? You can check your answer on page 46.

If you do not have a reciprocal key you will need to work out the division into 1 each time and store the answer in the memory.

More about reciprocals

A reciprocal is the mathematical name for the number you get when you divide a number into 1. For instance, the reciprocal of 2 is 0.5.

On some calculators the automatic constant divides numbers into 1 and you can use it to work out reciprocals. Press the keys shown above to see if it works on your calculator.*

Reciprocal trick

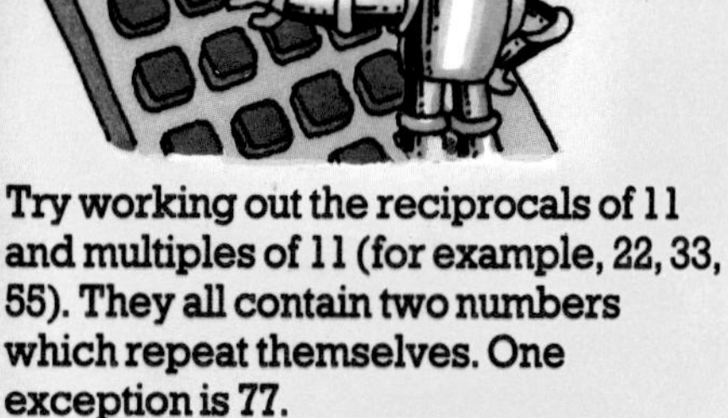

Try working out the reciprocals of 11 and multiples of 11 (for example, 22, 33, 55). They all contain two numbers which repeat themselves. One exception is 77.

Rearranging sums

$$\frac{7}{1.1 + 2.5}$$

If your calculator does not have memory keys you can use the reciprocal key to work out sums like the one shown above in one operation. To do it you need to rearrange the sum like this:

$$\frac{7}{1.1 + 2.5} = 7 \times \frac{1}{1.1 + 2.5}$$

[1] [•] [1] [+] [2] [•] [5]

[=] [1/x] [×] [7] [=] 1.9

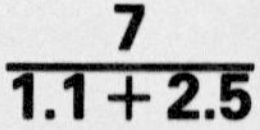

Then you can work out the bottom part of the fraction and press the reciprocal key and multiply by 7.

*If you get the answer 1, the automatic constant has divided 2 by itself, so you cannot use it to work out reciprocals.

Using the Pi key

Some calculators have a key labelled "π" (pronounced Pi). Pi is a never-ending number, discovered by the Ancient Greeks, which is used for working out the circumference and area of circles. Rounded off to seven decimal places it is 3.1415927.

Calculators with a π key have the number Pi stored in a special memory. When you want to use the number you can press the π key to put it into the display. If you have no π key and have to enter the number each time a shortened version, 3.14, is accurate enough for most calculations.

Working out circumferences

Working out areas

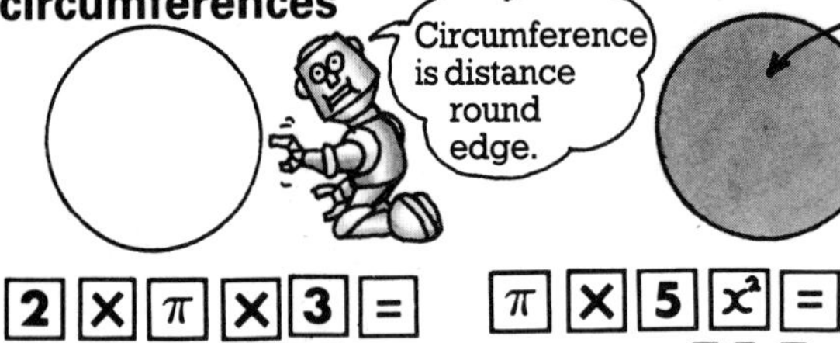

2 × π × 3 =

18.8 m

The mathematical formula for working out the circumference of a circle is $2\pi r$ (r stands for radius – the distance from the centre to the edge). Above are the keys to press to work out the circumference of a circle with a 3m radius.

π × 5 x^2 =

78.5 m^2

The formula for the area of a circle is πr^2. These are the keys to press to work out the area of a circle with a radius of 5m. If you do not have an x^2 key, enter the radius first, multiply it by itself and then multiply by π.

Walking the equator puzzle

How many steps would you take if you walked round the equator? Assume your steps are 0.5m long and use 6 370km as the radius of the Earth.

The answers are on page 46.

Bicycle puzzle

The robot's bicycle wheel is 66cm in diameter. How many times must it turn to travel 1km? (1km = 100 000cm).

If the wheel turns 120 times each minute, what is the bike's speed in km/h?

Petrol thieves puzzle

A gang of petrol thieves is at work while the tanker driver is asleep. There are 50 petrol cans to be filled and only 8 minutes before the police catch up with them. Each can measures 0.5m in diameter and 1m in height. The petrol flows out of the tanker at a rate of 900 litres per minute. Can they fill all the cans and get away in time?

(Answer on page 46.)

Vital information

The formula for working out the volume of a petrol can is $\pi r^2 \times h$ (h is the height of the can). This gives you the volume in cubic metres. Multiply it by 1 000 to convert it to litres.

Spheres

You also need π to work out the surface area and volume of spheres.

Surface area

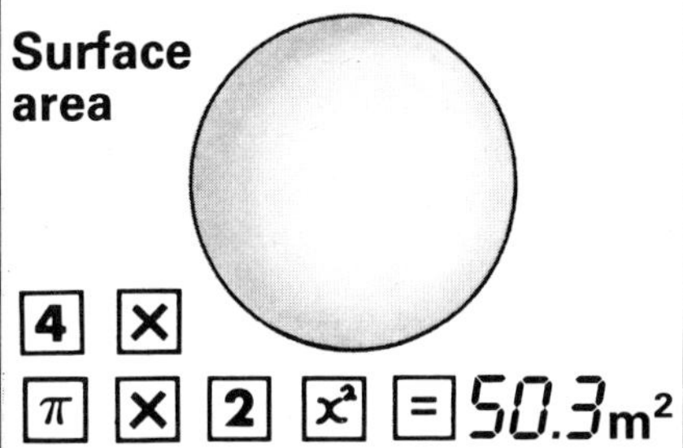

The formula for working out the surface area of a sphere is $4\pi r^2$. Above you can see how to use it for a sphere with a radius of 2m.

Volume

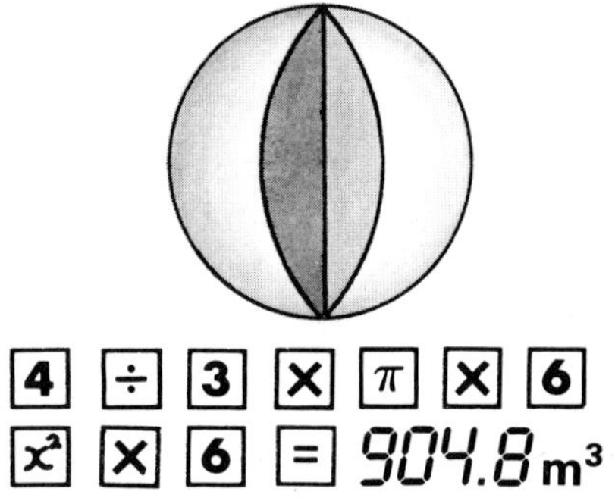

The formula for the volume of a sphere is $\frac{4}{3}\pi r^3$. The small 3 above the r means "cubed", that is, multiplied by itself three times. Here are the keys to press to find the volume of a sphere with a 6m radius.

Bubble puzzle

If the circumference of this bubble is 63mm, what is its surface area? (Answer on page 46.)

How to use a scientific calculator

A scientific calculator has lots of extra keys for complex mathematical functions. It can carry out these functions automatically because the rules for doing them are stored in the circuits of its permanent memory.

The keys and labels on scientific calculators vary a great deal and yours may not look exactly like the ones shown here. You may need to check how the keys on your calculator work in your instruction booklet.

Some calculators have no = key. These ► have an unusual system for entering numbers called Reverse Polish Notation (it was invented by a Polish mathematician). You enter all the numbers first, pressing a key marked "enter" after each number, then you press the appropriate function key.

Enter key

Inverse key

The display often has space for 10 or more digits on scientific calculators.

◄ Double function keys

Many of the keys on a scientific calculator do more than one job. To make a key perform its second function you have to press a key marked "2ndF" or "INV" (short for inverse). The label inverse is used on some calculators because the second function is often the opposite of the first. For example, squaring a number is the opposite of finding a square root, so these two functions are on the same key.

The symbols in red show the second function.

What numbers are missing from this calculation
93 × 8 = 7 8?
(Answer on page 46.)

Memory keys on scientific calculators

Many scientific calculators have an extra memory key called the memory exchange key. This swaps the number in the memory with the one in the display. It is labelled "MX" or "EXC". Some calculators, though, have completely different labels for the memory keys, as shown on the calculator on the left.

Memory store key

Memory recall key

Memory + key

Memory exchange key

This calculator has no memory clear key either. The number in the memory is automatically cleared when you store a new number using STO. Another way to clear the memory is to press C, then STO. This stores a zero in the memory.

▲ Long-term memory

In many scientific calculators the memory can store numbers for weeks or months, even when the calculator is switched off.

Using the constant on a scientific calculator

On scientific calculators the constant is not automatic. To bring it into action there is a special key labelled "K".

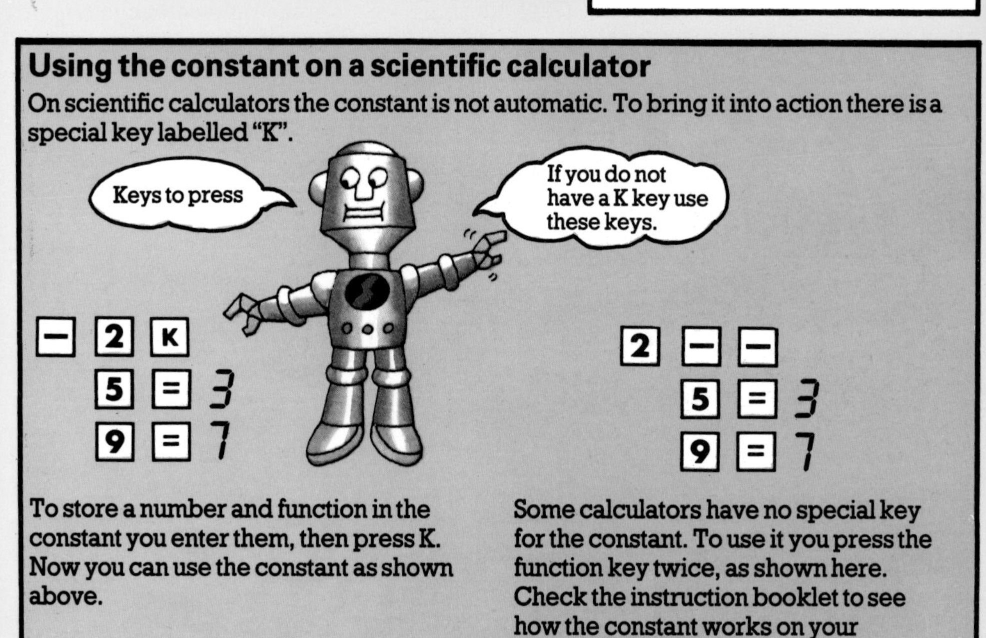

To store a number and function in the constant you enter them, then press K. Now you can use the constant as shown above.

Some calculators have no special key for the constant. To use it you press the function key twice, as shown here. Check the instruction booklet to see how the constant works on your calculator.

Calculator logic

When calculations have several parts they can have more than one answer. For example, the answer to $4 + 3 \times 2$ could be 14 (if you add $4 + 3$ first) or 10 (if you multiply 3×2 first). To avoid confusion mathematicians have rules for sums with several parts. These are: do the division parts first, then the multiplications, then additions, then subtractions. This order of working is called algebraic logic.

Some calculators use algebraic logic and will always do divisions and multiplications before additions and subtractions regardless of the order in which you enter the sum. To check whether your calculator uses algebraic logic enter $4 + 3 \times 2 =$. If it does, it will give the answer 10.

To change the order of a calculation mathematicians use brackets to show which parts should be worked out together.

1

$(137 + 7) \div 16$

In this sum the brackets show that you should work out the addition part before dividing by 16.

2

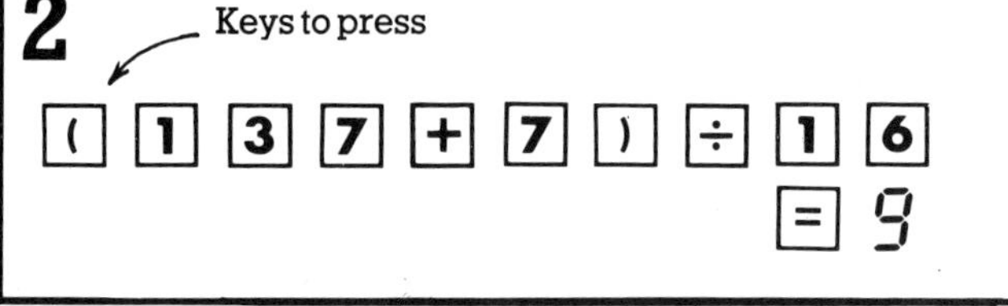

Scientific calculators have brackets keys, labelled (and), for doing calculations with brackets. You can see how to use them above. When you press the close bracket key the calculator works out the bit inside the brackets before going on.

Trying out the brackets keys

Here are some calculations you can do to try out the brackets keys. Where there are several sets of brackets in a calculation you should work out the functions between the sets of brackets in the correct mathematical order. A calculator with algebraic logic does this automatically so you can enter the sum in the order it is written. If your calculator does not use algebraic logic you must rearrange the sum and enter the different parts in the correct mathematical order.

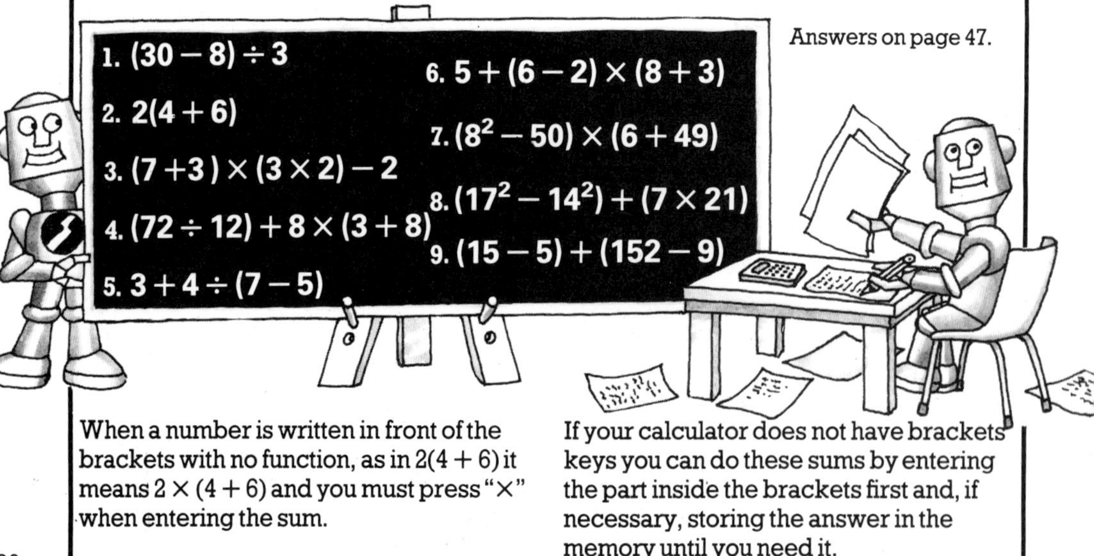

Answers on page 47.

When a number is written in front of the brackets with no function, as in $2(4 + 6)$ it means $2 \times (4 + 6)$ and you must press "×" when entering the sum.

If your calculator does not have brackets keys you can do these sums by entering the part inside the brackets first and, if necessary, storing the answer in the memory until you need it.

Nested brackets

$9 - 28 \div (70 \div (4 \times 2 + (3 - 1)))$

The calculation shown above has brackets within brackets. These are called nested brackets. If your calculator has brackets keys you can enter sums with nested brackets as shown below. The calculator automatically works them out in the correct mathematical order, which is to start with the innermost brackets and work outwards. You should work out the functions outside the brackets in the order of algebraic logic.

Most scientific calculators can cope with at least six sets of nested brackets. On some calculators a brackets symbol and a number are displayed each time you press the open brackets key, to show which set of brackets you are on.

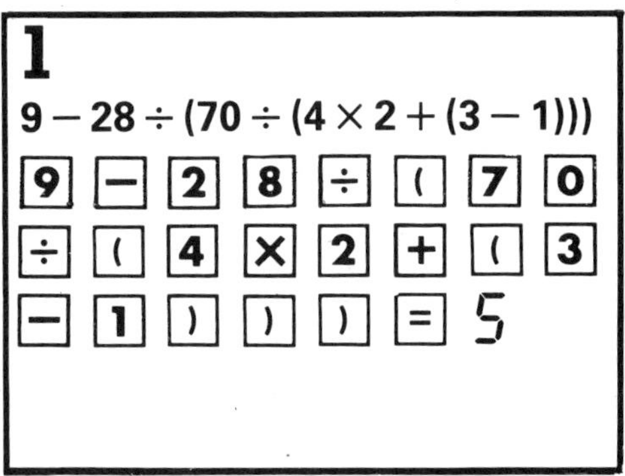

To do this calculation on a calculator with algebraic logic you enter it exactly as it is written and the calculator will work it out in the correct mathematical order.

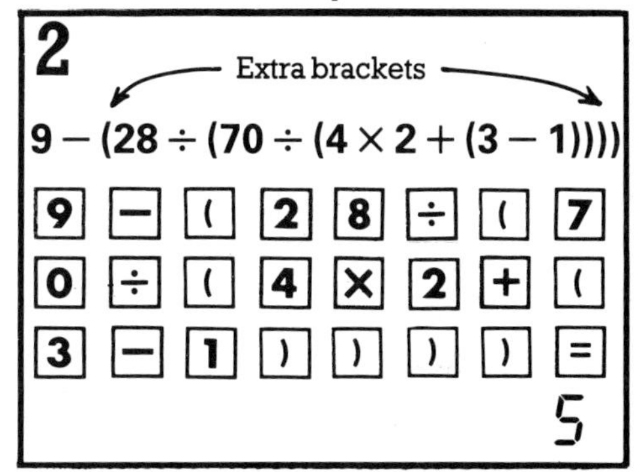

If your calculator does not use algebraic logic you must put in an extra set of brackets as shown above. This makes the calculator do the first division before the subtraction outside the brackets.

More calculations with brackets

Here are some examples you can do to practise using the nested brackets on your calculator. If your calculator does not have algebraic logic, remember to insert extra brackets where necessary so the calculations are worked out in the correct mathematical order. (Answers on page 47.)

1. $5 + 6(7 - (2 \times 3))$
2. $73(40^2 - (23 \times (64 \div 4))) + 7 \times (50 - (5 \times 8))$
3. $(9 + 4) \div 3(7 \div (2 + 8))$

A calculator with a game

This calculator has a built-in "speed-shoot" game, as well as the usual mathematical functions. To play it, you switch the calculator into a special mode using a key marked "game".

Numbers start to move across the display from the right. The aim of the game is to knock out each number before it reaches the left-hand side and destroys one of your defences. You have an "aim" key which you have to press nine times to aim for a 9, three times for a 3 and so on, and a "fire" key. When all three defences are destroyed the game is over.

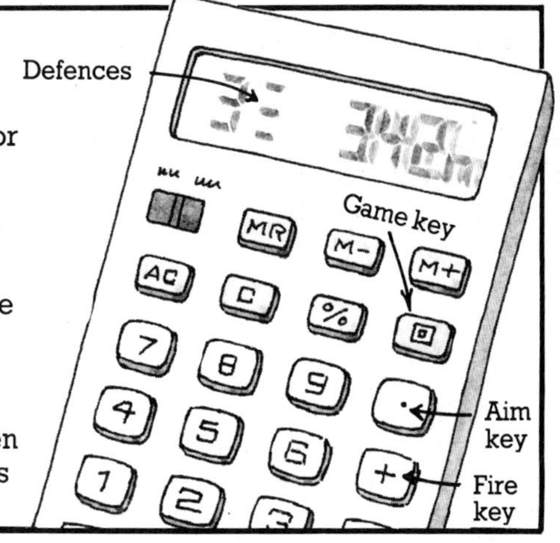

Angles and triangles

The keys labelled "tan", "sin" and "cos" (short for tangent, sine and cosine) are for working out measurements on right-angled triangles. They enable you to work out the lengths of the sides if you only know one angle and a side. To use these keys you enter the size of an angle, say 50°, then press the tan, cos or sin key.

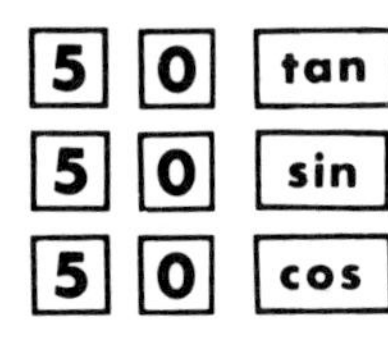

1.1917536

0.7660444

0.6427876

On some calculators it takes a moment for the answer to appear because the calculator needs "thinking time".*

To work out the measurements of a right-angled triangle there are some mathematical formulae using the tan, cos or sin of an angle.

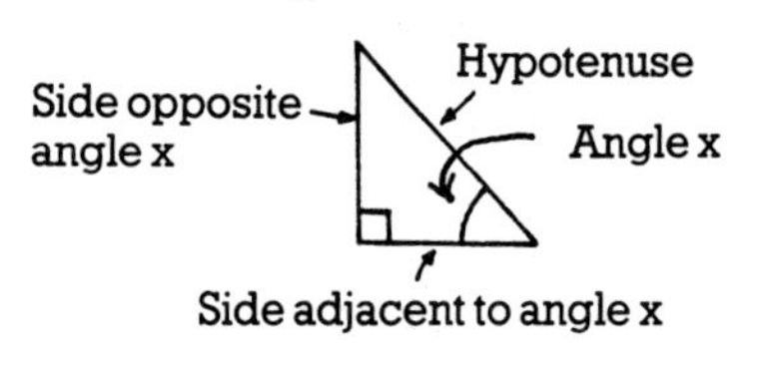

1. $\frac{\text{Opposite side}}{\text{Adjacent side}} = \tan x$

2. $\frac{\text{Opposite side}}{\text{Hypotenuse}} = \sin x$

3. $\frac{\text{Adjacent side}}{\text{Hypotenuse}} = \cos x$

You can find out how to use these formulae below.

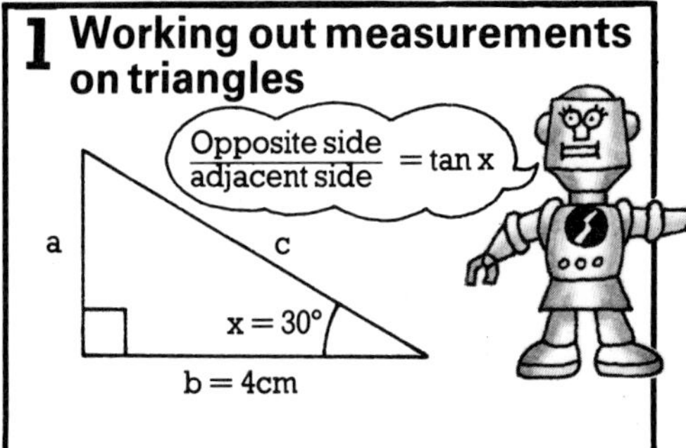

On this triangle angle x is 30° and its adjacent side, b, is 4cm. To work out the length of side a (opposite side) you can use formula 1.

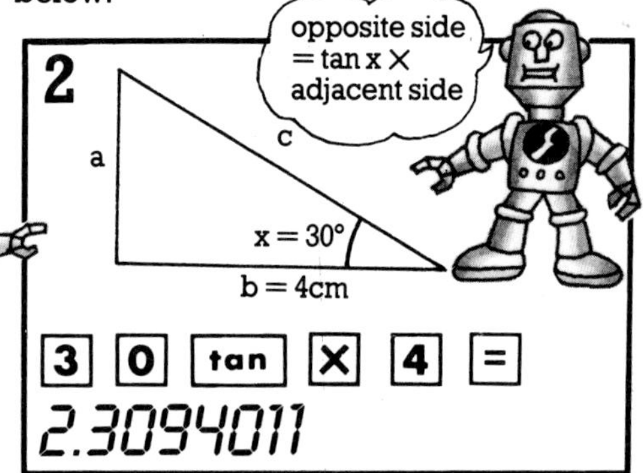

You know two of the measurements in the formula, so by turning the equation round you can work out that a (opposite side) = tan 30° × 4 (adjacent side).

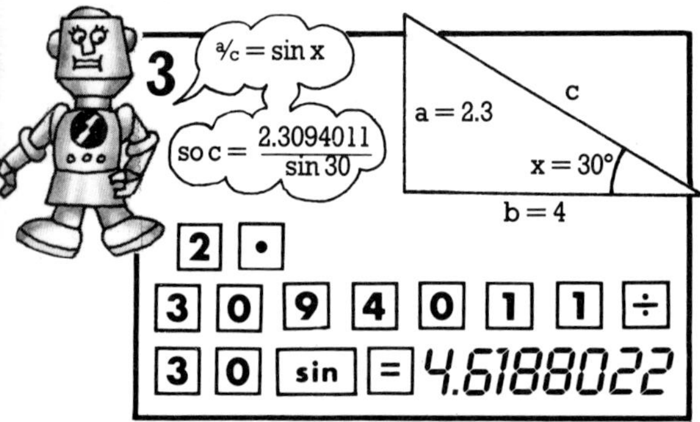

Now that you know the length of two of the sides you can work out the hypotenuse using formula 2 or 3. Do not round off the answer for side a if you use it in this calculation. The keys to press for formula 2 are shown above.

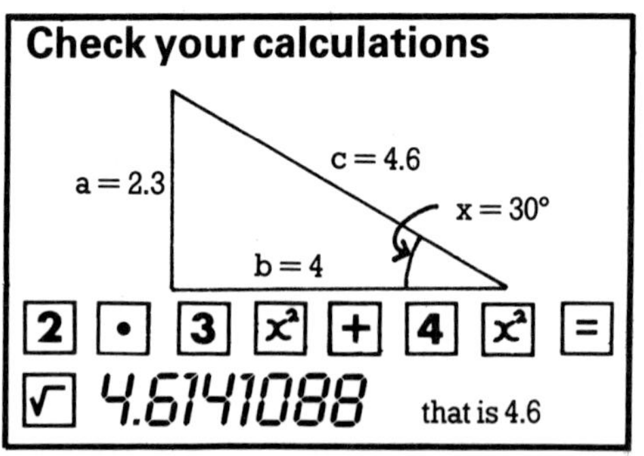

Now that you have worked out all the sides of the triangle you can check your calculations using Pythagoras' theorem (see page 24). According to this, $a^2 + b^2 = c^2$. The keys to press for this calculation are shown above.

*If your answers are different from those above read the note on "Working in degrees" on the opposite page.

Yachtsman puzzle

A yachtsman on a stormy sea wants to find out how far he is from a dangerous headland. He works out that, from where he is, the beam of light from the lighthouse makes an angle of 40° with the sea level. The lighthouse is 45m high and is standing on a cliff 30m above sea level. How far is he from the headland? The answer is on page 47.

Hint

The top of the lighthouse, the yacht and the headland make the points of a right-angled triangle.

Working in degrees

Angles are usually measured in degrees (° is the symbol for degrees), but they can be measured in two other sets of units, just as length can be measured in metres or yards. The other units are called radians and gradients. One radian is 57.3° and one gradient is 0.9°.

On most scientific calculators there is a key or switch labelled "D.R.G", which sets the calculator to work in whichever unit you want. Each time you press the D.R.G key the unit changes and a symbol or letters (usually DEG, RAD or GRA) appear to show which units are being used. Make sure the calculator is using the correct units before you start doing calculations with angles.

Degrees can be subdivided into minutes and seconds. Some calculators have an extra key for entering degrees, minutes and seconds.

Working backwards

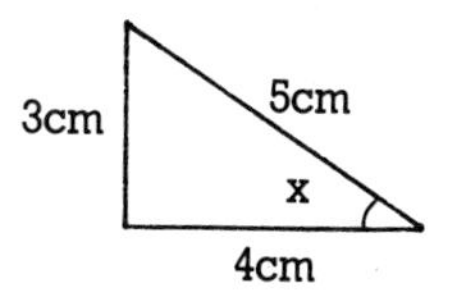

Sometimes you know the lengths of the sides of a triangle, and want to work out its angles. You can do this using the mathematical formulae given previously. On this triangle the sides measure 3cm, 4cm and 5cm. You can find angle x using any of the formulae. If you use formula 1,

$$\frac{\text{opposite side (3)}}{\text{adjacent side (4)}} = \tan x$$

So $\tan x = 0.75$.

Your answer is the tan of x. You can convert this to an angle by pressing the inverse key* and then the tan key. The keys to press are shown here.

0 • 7 5 INV tan

You could also find x by working out its sine or cosine. $\sin x = 3/5 = 0.6$ and $\cos x = 4/5 = 0.8$, so to work out x the keys to press are:

0 • 6 INV sin

0 • 8 INV cos

*Some calculators have a key labelled "ARC" which you use with the sin, cos and tan keys instead of the inverse key.

Working out powers and roots

Multiplying a number by itself over and over again is called raising it to a power. For example, if you multiply 4 by itself five times, that is, $4 \times 4 \times 4 \times 4 \times 4$ you are raising it to the power 5. The power shows how many times the number appears in the multiplication. It is written 4^5.

Raising a number to the power 2 is the same as squaring it. Raising it to the power 3 is called cubing it.

Most scientific calculators have a key for working out powers, labelled y^x (y is the number you want to multiply and x is the power).*

Above you can see the keys to press to work out 4^5. Try out the power key on these numbers too: 9^8, 15^3, 6^1, 12^4, 5^7. The answers are on page 47.

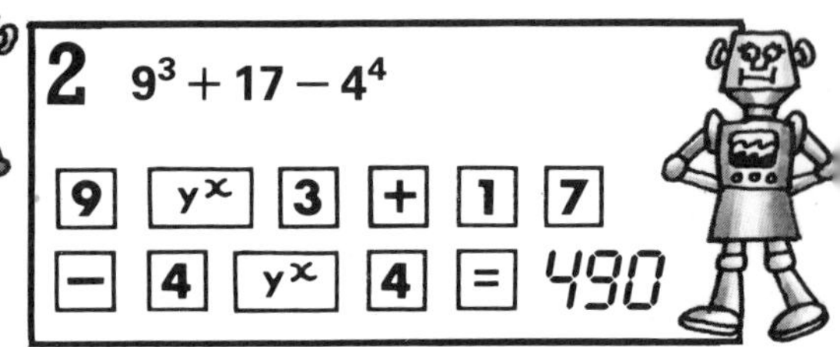

You can usually work out powers in sums as you go along. Remember, the +, −, × and ÷ keys act as = keys so you do not need to press = until the end of the sum.

To do this sum work out everything inside the brackets first, then raise the result to the power of 7. Above you can see how to do it using the brackets keys (see page 31).

Negative powers

The number 4^{-3} is called a negative power. You can work out negative powers on a calculator using the change sign key.

4 yˣ 3 +/− = 0.015625

In fact 4^{-3} is the same as $\frac{1}{4}^3$. Another way to work it out is to do 4^3, then divide the answer into 1 by pressing the reciprocal key as shown below.

4 yˣ 3 = 1/x 0.015625

3^{-4} 5^{-2} 4^{-1} 6^{-5}

Try working out these negative powers. The answers are on page 47.

Working out roots

Roots are the opposite of powers. For example, $4^5 = 1024$ and the 5th root of 1024 is 4. Roots can be written in two ways: $\sqrt[5]{1024}$ or $1024^{1/5}$.

Some calculators have a root key labelled $\sqrt[x]{y}$ or $y^{1/x}$, but on many the root function is on the same key as the power function. To work out a root on these calculators you press the inverse key before pressing the power key, as shown on the right.

Above you can see the keys to press to work out the 5th root of 32. Can you work out the other roots? The answers are on page 47.

*On some calculators the label is x^y – so x is the number and y the power.

Taking risks

Is it worth taking a risk? There is a mathematical way to work out how big a risk you are taking and what your chances are of winning. Say someone bets that they can cut a newly shuffled pack of cards and get the ace of spades. You can work out their chances of winning as follows. There are 52 cards in the pack and only one of them is the ace of spades, so their chances of winning are 1 in 52. You can write this as $1/52$ or as a decimal 0.019. If you convert the decimal to a fraction it is $19/1000$, so you should get the ace 19 times out of every thousand cuts.

Now try this one. If you toss a coin five times, what are your chances of getting five heads in a row.

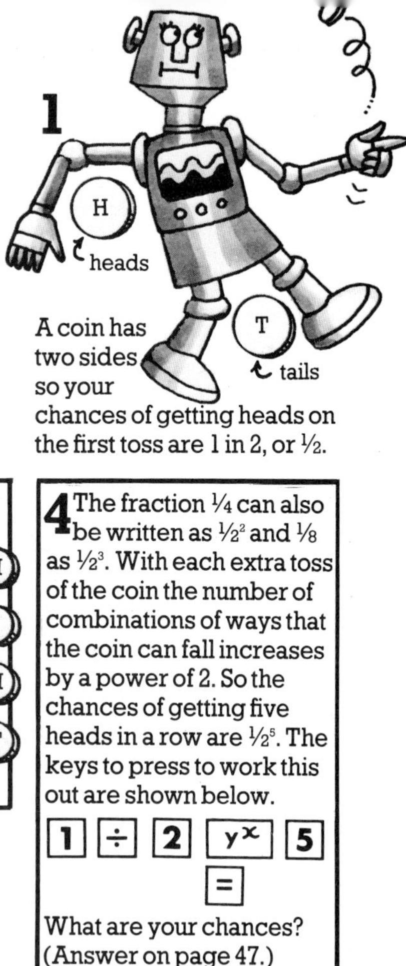

1 A coin has two sides so your chances of getting heads on the first toss are 1 in 2, or $1/2$.

2 Possible combinations for two tosses.

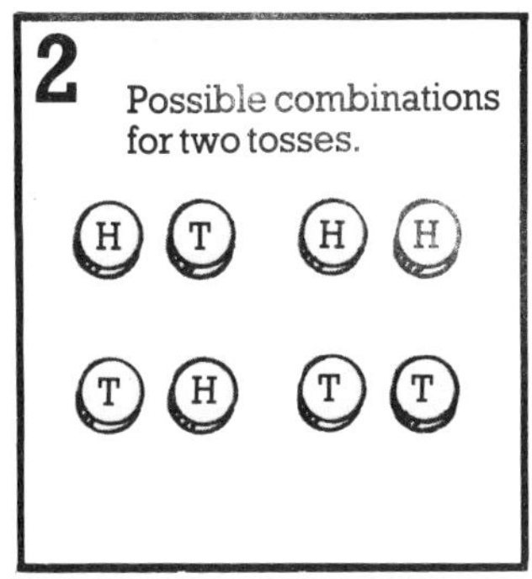

For two tosses there are four possible combinations of heads and tails. Only one of them is H, H, so your chances of getting two heads in a row are $1/4$.

3 Possible combinations for three tosses.

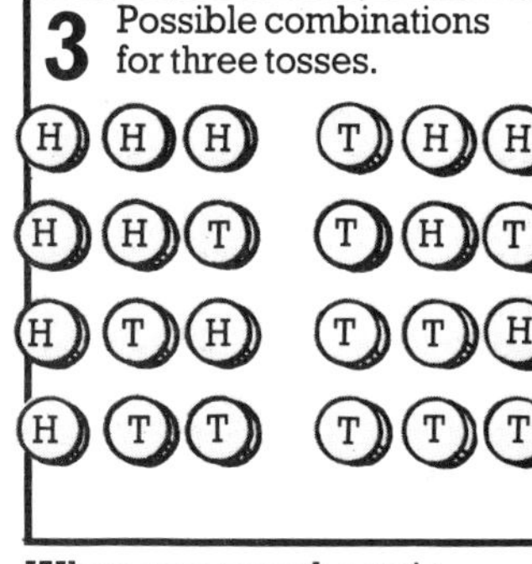

When you toss the coin three times in a row there are eight possible combinations of heads and tails. Your chances of getting three heads are $1/8$.

4 The fraction $1/4$ can also be written as $1/2^2$ and $1/8$ as $1/2^3$. With each extra toss of the coin the number of combinations of ways that the coin can fall increases by a power of 2. So the chances of getting five heads in a row are $1/2^5$. The keys to press to work this out are shown below.

[1] [÷] [2] [y^x] [5] [=]

What are your chances? (Answer on page 47.)

Calculators in space

Space shuttle pilots take special calculators with them for doing complex calculations during the flights.

The calculators are programmable. In fact, they are like small computers with displays which show words as well as numbers.

The shuttle pilots take two calculators. One is programmed to work out which ground station the pilots can contact at every stage in the mission, and when and for how long the contact can be made. The second is for working out how the spacecraft should be balanced for re-entry into the Earth's atmosphere.

Very large and very small numbers

Simple calculators cannot cope with numbers so large or so small that they have too many digits to fit into the display. However scientific calculators can do sums with these numbers using a kind of shorthand called scientific notation.

If you do this multiplication, the calculator gives the answer as shown above. The answer is in scientific notation and it means 8.84×10^{11}. The 10^{11} part is called the exponent.

The exponent shows how many places you move the decimal point to change the answer to an ordinary number. In this case you move it 11 places to the right. (This is the same as multiplying 8.84 by 10^{11}.)

To see what the calculator does with a very small number, try dividing 1 by 80 000 000. The calculator gives the answer in scientific notation and it means 1.25×10^{-8}.

When the exponent is negative you move the decimal point to the left. In this case you move the point eight places to the left as shown above. (This is the same as multiplying 1.25 by 10^{-8}.)

Sun puzzle

The Sun is 1.5×10^{11} metres away from Earth and the speed of light is 3×10^{8}m/sec. How long does it take light from the Sun to reach Earth? Give the answer in seconds. (You can check your answers to these puzzles on page 47.)

Snail puzzle

If a snail moves at 0.0005km/h, how long would it take it to crawl to the Moon 384 000km away? Give your answer in years.

Doing sums in scientific notation

You can also use scientific notation to do calculations with numbers which are too large for the display. You have to enter the numbers in scientific notation and you can do this using an exponent key labelled "EXP" or "EE".

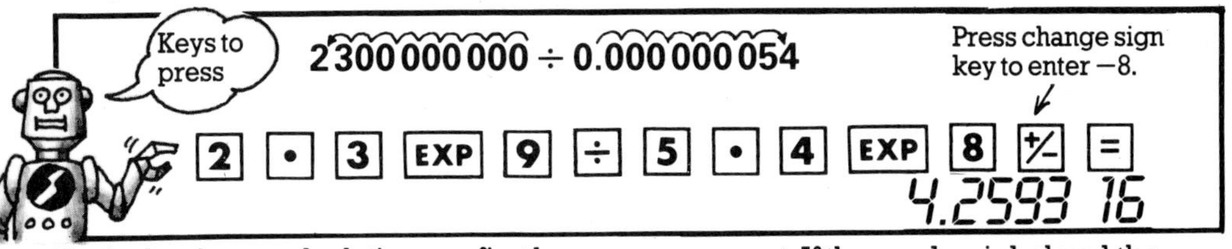

To do the above calculation you first have to convert the numbers to scientific notation. To convert numbers above 1, you move the decimal point to the left until it comes after the first digit. To convert numbers below 1, you move the decimal point to the right until it comes after the first digit which is above 0. The number of times you move the decimal point is the exponent. If the number is below 1 the exponent is negative.

In the first number you move the point nine times to the left, so the scientific notation is 2.3×10^9. In the second number you move the point eight times to the right so the scientific notation is 5.4×10^{-8}. The keys to press to enter these numbers are shown above.

Examples to try

1. $650\,000\,000 \times 342\,000 \times 3\,098$

2. $1\,376\,000\,000 \div 0.000\,000\,08$

3. $8\,052\,000\,000 \times 23 \div 0.000\,000\,55$

Here are some more examples to try using scientific notation. If a number is small enough to fit into the display you can enter it in the normal way. Calculators which use scientific notation can cope with a mixture of scientific and ordinary numbers. (Answers on page 47.)

Unexpected answers

$(7.45 \times 10^{10}) + 23$

See if you can do this example on a calculator. In its answer the calculator appears not to have added 23. This is because when you are dealing with such a large number 23 is too small a part of it to show up. In fact the answer is 74 500 000 023, but the nearest the calculator can get to it is 7.45×10^{10}.

Paper folding puzzle

Try to guess the answer to this puzzle before you work it out.

If you had a sheet of paper 0.15mm thick and folded it in half 50 times* how high would it be?

Hint

You have to double 0.15mm 50 times, which is the same as multiplying it by 2^{50}.

*In fact this is impossible. A square sheet of paper cannot be folded more than eight times – try it and see.

Simple statistics

Statistics are facts and figures which give information about groups of things. One way of giving information about groups is to work out an average. The mathematical term for an average is an "arithmetic mean".

Some calculators have special keys for working out averages and other kinds of statistics. The keys are labelled differently on different calculators. The most common labels are shown here, but check the instruction booklet to find the statistics keys on your calculator.

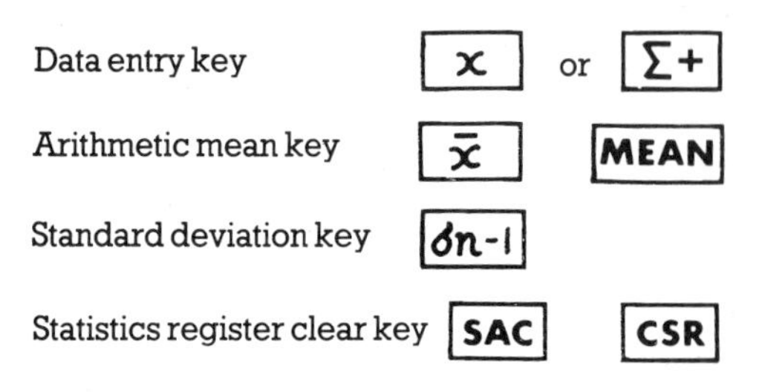

These are the basic statistics keys, with the labels most frequently used. On some calculators you have to switch into a statistics register or "mode" before you can do statistics. When you are using the statistics keys other functions, such as the memory, may be out of action because the calculator needs them itself.

Using the statistics keys

To find out how to use the statistics keys try working out the average time of these six runners in a 100 metre race. The times are your "data" and they are shown in the picture below.

12.1secs

11.8secs

10.4secs

10.5secs

11.2secs

9.7secs

Data entry key

9 • 7 Σ+ 1 0 • 4 Σ+ 1 0 • 5 Σ+ 1 1 • 2 Σ+ 1 1 • 8 Σ+ 1 2 • 1 Σ+ MEAN 10.95

Arithmetic mean key

To work out the average time, you add all the times, then divide by the number of runners. To do this on a calculator switch to the statistics register (if necessary) then press the statistics register clear key to make sure that there are no numbers left there from previous calculations. Enter the times of the runners using the data entry key. The keys to press are shown above. Then press the arithmetic mean key to make the calculator work out the average and show it in the display.

Entering data

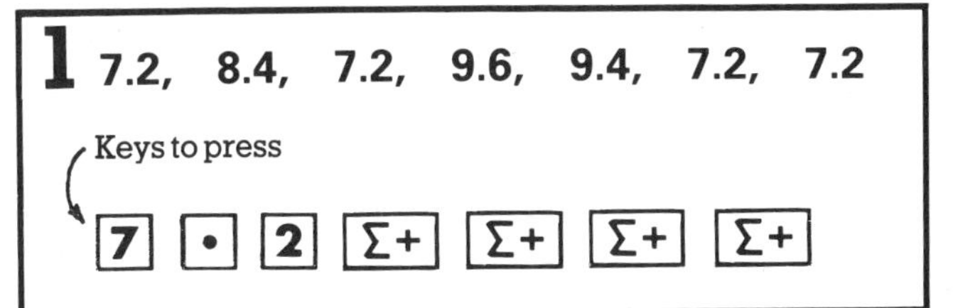

2

3 • 8 C

3 • 9 or Σ−

When you have lots of data some of the figures may be the same. In the example above you can group the figures so all the 7.2s can be entered together. To enter the figures, press the digit keys once, then press the data entry key the number of times the figure occurs.

If you enter a number wrongly, you can clear it by pressing the usual clear entry key, or a special Σ− or "DEL" key.

More about averages

Averages may give misleading information if one or two of the figures on which they are based are much higher or lower than the rest. If the slowest runner took 23.4 instead of 12.1 seconds, the new average time would be 12.8 seconds. This is slower than five of the six runners, so it does not give a true picture of the speed of the race.

Mathematicians have a way of working out how much figures vary from the average. It is called finding the "standard deviation" of the average. The key for doing it on a calculator is labelled σn-1.

23.4secs

11.8secs

11.2secs

10.4secs

10.5secs

9.7secs

Working out standard deviations

To work out a standard deviation, enter all the data then press the standard deviation key. Try it with the runners' times in the first example. (You should get 0.91secs.)

Now try the standard deviation for the second example. A higher figure for the standard deviation shows that the data is spread over a wider range.

Other statistics keys

Some calculators have several more statistics keys, such as the "sum of data squared" key labelled Σx^2 which is for more complex statistical calculations.

You may also have an Σx key which gives the sum of all the data entered and a key labelled "n" which you can press to check the number of data you entered. Some calculators automatically display a running total as you enter the data.

Permutations

In the picture on the right there are three robots and three seats. How many different arrangements of robots on seats do you think there are?

Different arrangements of things are called permutations. There is a mathematical way to work out how many permutations are possible. You can find out what it is below.

How to work it out

For the first seat there are three possible robots. For the second seat there are two possible robots in each case, and for the third seat there is one possible robot in each case. To work out the number of different seating arrangements you multiply the number of possible robots for each seat, that is 3 × 2× 1.

Working it out on a calculator

The calculation 3 × 2 × 1 is a "factorial". It is called factorial 3 and is written 3!. Most scientific calculators have a key for working out factorials, labelled x! or n!. You can see how to use it above.

If there were seven robots and seven seats the number of possibilities for the first seat would be 7, for the second, 6, and so on. So the number of permutations would be 7!.

Choosing a space crew

Marlo wants a new crew for the spaceship. He needs three crew members and there are 17 to choose from. How many different crews could he have?

1 7 × 1 6 × 1 5 ÷ 3 x! =

You need to find out how many combinations of three you can get from 17. Then you must take into account that some of these will be different permutations of the same three (ABC is the same as BAC, BCA, and so on). To work out how many *different* groups of three are possible, you have to divide the total number of combinations by the number of possible permutations of 3.

The total number of combinations is 17 × 16 × 15, because there are 17 possibilities for the first crew member, 16 possibilities for the second crew member and 15 for the third crew member. Divide this by the number of permutations of 3 that are possible, that is 3!, to get the answer. You should find that Marlo can have 680 different crews.

Picking teams

Imagine you have to pick two football teams of 11 people. There are 15 boys and 20 girls to choose from. How many different boys' and how many different girls' teams could you make? (Answers on page 47.)

Statistics puzzle

There are six statistics puzzles in this picture. Can you solve them? (When you work out an average give the standard deviation too.) The answers are on page 47.

1 What is the average number of people at a bus-stop?

2 If one bus queue waits three minutes for a bus, another waits 20 minutes and the third waits half an hour, what is the average time each queue waits for a bus?

3 What percentage of the people are waiting for a bus and what percentage are travelling by car?

4 How many different combinations of people from this queue could sit on the seat in the bus-stop? (The seat holds four people.)

5 These men are erecting three statues. How many different ways could they arrange them?

6 What are the chances of two people in this picture having the same birthday?
You can find out how to work this out below.

Birthday puzzle

In order to work this out you need to find out the probability of people having different birthdays, then turn the answer round, to find out the probability of them having the same birthday.

There are 365 possible birthdays and 31 people in the picture. For one person the probability of another having a different birthday is 364/365, the probability of a third person having a different birthday from the first two is 363/365, and so on for all the 30 people. To work out the chances of everyone having different birthdays you multiply all the probabilities together, that is

$$\frac{364}{365} \times \frac{363}{365} \times \frac{362}{365} \times \frac{361}{365} \cdots\cdots \frac{335}{365}$$

To do this, multiply the top parts of the fraction, then divide by 365^{30}.

3 6 4 × 3 6 3 × 3 6 2 . . . × 3 3 5 ÷ 3 6 5 y^x 3 0 = 0.2695454

The answer is 0.27, which is 27%. So the probability of everyone having different birthdays is 27%. That means the probability of two people having the same birthday is 100 − 27 = 73%.

Other keys

Some scientific calculators have lots more keys not mentioned so far. Two of the most common are the logarithm, or log, keys labelled "log" and "ln". The log key gives the common logarithm of a number, that is, the number expressed as a power of 10. For example, 100 is 10^2, so log 100 is 2. The "ln" key gives the natural logarithm of a number. A natural logarithm is a number expressed as a power of this number: 2.7182818 (this number is called "e").

Logs were invented before calculators existed to make multiplying and dividing long numbers easier. Instead of multiplying you can add their logs and instead of dividing you can subtract their logs. Logs are still used in some scientific calculations.

A key marked a b/c is for doing calculations with fractions without changing them to decimals.

Using the common log key

To get the common log of a number you enter it, then press the log key as shown above.

2 INV log 100

The log key usually has an "antilog" function on it too. This converts logs back to ordinary numbers. To use it, enter the log and press the inverse key, then the log key. The symbol for a common antilog is "10^x"

Using the natural log key

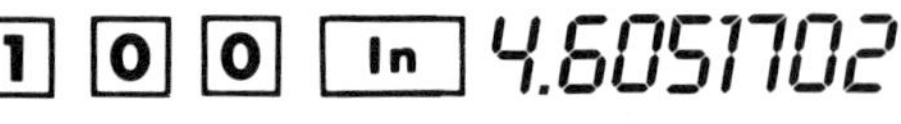

To find the natural log of a number you enter it, then press the ln key.

The symbol for a natural antilog is "e^x". You can find natural antilogs using the inverse key as shown above. (The answer in this case may not be 100 because you entered a rounded off version of log 100.)

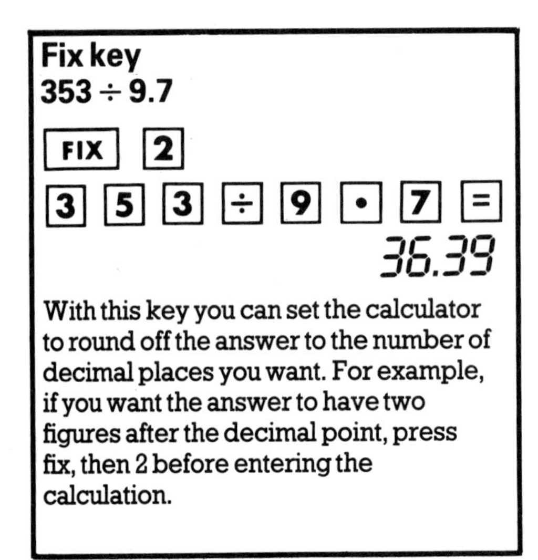

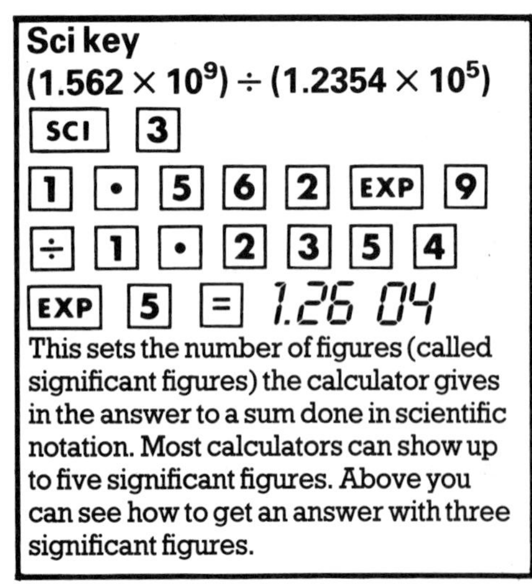

Puzzle answers

Most of the answers are rounded off to whole numbers or one decimal place. Where it is necessary to be more accurate the answer is given as it would appear on a calculator with an eight-digit display which rounds off the last digit.

If you have rounded off numbers before the end of a sum, your final answer may be slightly different from the ones given.

Page 2

The largest number you can produce is 22412, that is 431×52.

Page 4

You can make the calculator display 50 using only 7, 5, +, − and = by doing the following calculation:
$7+7+7+7+7+7+7+7(=56)-5$ $(=51)+7+7(=65)-5-5-5=50$.
Or you can just enter 55−5. Can you think of any other ways?

Page 6
Simple sums

$25 \times 4 = 100$; $1100 \times 9 + 9 = 9909$;
$30 \div 2.4 - 3 = 9.5$; $9521 - 4193 = 5328$;
$10.4 \div 2 = 5.2$; $6400 \div 8 = 800$;
$6 \times 10 \times 100 = 6000$; $9 + 17 = 26$;
$54 \div 4.5 - 6 = 6$; $700 \times 4.3 \div 301 = 10$;
$805.2 - 605.2 = 200$; $4098 - 3097 = 1001$;
$6059 \times 423 = 2562957$

Page 7
Rough guesses

$512 \times 359 = 183808$ (rough guess = 200000)
$971 \times 28 = 27188$ (rough guess = 30000)
$1594 + 273 = 1867$ (rough guess = 1900)
$6123 \div 57 = 107.4$ (rough guess = $6000 \div 60$)

Page 8
Car rally puzzle

Your average speed over the last section must be just over 98km/h. So it is unlikely that you can reach the check-point in time without breaking the speed limit.

The other car's average speed is almost 47km/h. That is the total distance (19.5km) divided by the time it takes ($25 \div 60$ hours).

Page 9
Converting fractions

$1/10 = 0.1$; $7\,3/4 = 7.75$; $3\,5/8 = 3.625$;
$9/8 = 1.125$; $5/17 = 0.2941176$;
$15/16 = 0.9375$; $21\,2/3 = 21.666667$

Page 13
Binary decoder

0011 = 3; 1111 = 15; 0101 = 5;
0111 = 7; 1100 = 12; 1001 = 9.

Page 14
Calculator versus brain race

$4 \times 12 = 48$; $9 + 46 = 55$; $175 - 50 = 125$;
$70 \times 5 = 350$; $108 \div 12 = 9$; $4 \times 7 + 5 = 33$;
$9 + 8 - 3 = 14$; $73 - 17 + 16 = 72$;
$244 \div 2 + 15 = 137$; $2 \times 2 + 46 = 50$

Page 17
Mountaineer puzzle

The mountaineer can take 13 bars of chocolate. One way to work this out is to calculate the weight (in kg) that he has already:

$$11.75 + 2 + (2 \times 0.43) + (7 \times 0.085) + (3 \times 0.113) + (5 \times 0.021)$$

Doing the additions in the memory will give you an MR total of 15.649. Subtract this from 17kg to find out how much more weight he can take, then divide by 0.103 to work out how many bars of chocolate that is.

Page 18
Conversions

15 miles = 24.1km
45 miles = 72.4km
66 miles = 106.2km
105 miles = 168.9km

Page 19
Space invader puzzle

You have not beaten your friend. The difference between your scores is 1,910 points. The best way to work it out is to calculate each part of your score and add them in the memory. Then you can press MR to find out your total score. To find the difference between the scores enter your friend's score and subtract yours from it by pressing "−", then MR.

Page 20

Hats puzzle

44% (4/9) of the robots have yellow hats, 33% (3/9) have red hats and 22% (2/9) have blue hats.

Page 21

Galactic spore puzzle

The scientists of Zanof have five days in which to find a herbicide. On the sixth day the planet will be completely overrun. Your calculations should show:

day 1	20 + 33% = 26.6% of planet covered
day 2	+ 33% = 35.378%
day 3	+ 33% = 47.05274%
day 4	+ 33% = 65.5801442%
day 5	+ 33% = 83.231592%
day 6	+ 33% = 110.69802%

Percentages without a % key

25% of 5 800 = 1 450; 35% of 675 = 236.25; 115% of 50 = 57.5; 46% of 900 = 414.

Page 22-23

Doing squares

$11^2 = 121$; $42^2 = 1764$; $94^2 = 8836$; $103^2 = 10609$.

$0.2^2 = 0.04$; $0.65^2 = 0.4225$; $0.83^2 = 0.6889$; $0.9^2 = 0.81$.

Reappearing squares

The three other numbers which, when squared, reappear as the last figures in the answer are $76^2 = 5776$; $376^2 = 141376$; $625^2 = 390625$.

Doing square roots

$\sqrt{15} = 3.9$; $\sqrt{88} = 9.4$; $\sqrt{529} = 23$; $\sqrt{1944} = 44.1$

$2 \times \sqrt{324} \div 3 = 12$;
$3 \times \sqrt{1089} - \sqrt{4356} = 33$;
$9555 \div \sqrt{5402.25} = 130$

Page 24

Slim Sally's CB aerial

Each guy rope is 6.7m long.

Walking puzzle

Lee has walked 13.9km.

Star warrior puzzle

It takes 6.5 minutes for the chamber to fill with water, so the rescuers arrive just in time.

Page 26

Walking the equator p

It would take just over 80 m walk the equator.

Bicycle puzzle

The bicycle wheel must turn 482 times to travel 1km. If it turns 120 times each minute its speed is 15kph.

To work out these two answers you need to find the distance the wheel travels in 1 turn, that is, its circumference. Divide by 100 000 to convert the distance to km, then divide the result into 1 to find the number of turns necessary to travel 1km.

To work out the bike's speed if the wheel turns 120 times each minute, multiply 120 by 60 to find out the number of turns in an hour, then divide by 482 (the number of turns in 1km) to work out the speed in km/h.

Petrol thieves puzzle

The thieves cannot get away in time. It takes almost 11 minutes to fill the 50 cans with petrol.

To work this out, you need to find the volume of one can (in cubic metres) and multiply by 1000 to convert it to litres. Then multiply by 50 to find the total amount of petrol they need, and divide the answer by the rate of flow (900 litres per minute) to find out how long it takes to fill the cans.

Page 27

Bubble puzzle

The surface area of the bubble is 1 263mm^2.

One way to work it out is to find the radius of the bubble by dividing the circumference by 2π, then square the answer and multiply by 4π to find the surface area.

Page 28

The calculation with missing numbers should be $93 \times 86 = 7998$

Page 30
Trying out the brackets keys
1. 7.3; **2.** 20; **3.** 58; **4.** 94; **5.** 5; **6.** 49; **7.** 770; **8.** 240; **9.** 153

Page 31
More calculations with brackets
1. 11; **2.** 90 006; **3.** 3.03

Page 33
Yachtsman puzzle
The yacht is 89.4m from the lighthouse. The height of the cliff and lighthouse is the side opposite the angle of 40° and the yacht's distance from the headland is the side adjacent to the angle. So you can work out the distance using the formula

$$\tan 40° = \frac{\text{opposite side}}{\text{adjacent side}}$$

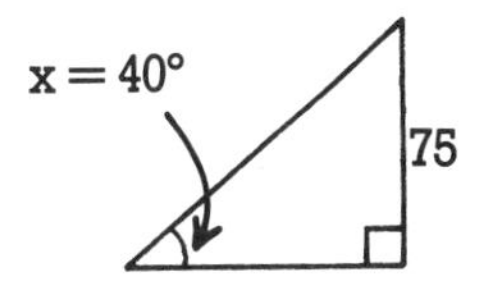

$$\tan 40° = \frac{75}{\text{distance}}, \quad \text{so distance} = \frac{75}{\tan 40°}$$

Page 34
Using the power key
$9^8 = 43\,046\,721$; $15^3 = 3\,375$; $6^1 = 6$; $12^4 = 20\,736$; $5^7 = 78\,125$

Negative powers
$3^{-4} = 0.0123457$; $5^{-2} = 0.04$; $4^{-1} = 0.25$; $6^{-5} = 0.0001286$

Working out roots
$\sqrt[8]{6\,561} = 3$; $\sqrt[7]{16\,384} = 4$; $\sqrt[5]{3\,125} = 5$

Page 35
Taking risks
The chances of getting five heads in a row are 0.03125, that is approximately 3/100, or three in every hundred attempts.

Pages 36-37
Sums in scientific notation
1. 6.8869×10^{17}
2. 1.72×10^{16}
3. 3.3672×10^{17}

Pages 36-37
Sun puzzle
It takes 500 seconds (that is just over 8 minutes) for light from the Sun to reach Earth.

Snail puzzle
It would take the snail 87 671 years to reach the Moon. That is 7.68×10^8 hours divided by the number of hours in a year (24×365).

Paper folding puzzle
The paper would be 1.6888×10^8km high. That is more than 168 million km – right out into space, beyond the Sun.

You can work out 0.15×2^{50} using the power key, or if you want to see how the height of the paper increases, you can enter × 2 in the constant, then enter 0.15 and press = fifty times. Both methods give you the answer in mm, so divide by 1 000 000 to convert it to km.

Page 41
Picking teams
You could choose 1 365 different boys' teams and 167 960 different girls' teams.

Pages 42-43
Statistics puzzle
1. The average number of people at a bus-stop is 6, with a standard deviation of 4.6 people.

2. The average length of time waited by each queue is 17.7 minutes with a standard deviation of 13.7 minutes.

3. Of the people in the picture 58% (18/31) are travelling by bus and 13% (4/31) are travelling by car.

4. The number of different combinations of people who could sit in the seat is 330, that is $11 \times 10 \times 9 \times 8 \div 4!$

5. There are 6 possible ways of arranging the three figures in the statue.

Index

First published 1982 by Usborne Publishing Ltd, 20 Garrick Street, London WC2 9BJ, England.